D1097196

PKO Poker Strategy

Dara O'Kearney

with

Barry Carter

PKO Poker Strategy

Copyright © 2020 Barry Carter and Dara O'Kearney

All rights reserved. No part of this book may be reproduced or transmitted in any forms or by any means, without written permission from the authors, except for the inclusion of brief quotations in a review. To request permission to use any part of the book in any way email: **barryrichardcarter@gmail.com**.

Cover design by Tiger-Fruit, https://www.tiger-fruit.com/

Dara's headshot courtesy of Tambet Kask and Unibet Poker.

www.dokearney.blogspot.com
www.pokermediapro.com

INDEX

Assumptions

To get the most out of this book, we have made some assumptions about how familiar you are with some key concepts in poker. If you are unfamiliar with any of the following assumptions it is perhaps best to do a bit of independent research to bring you up to speed.

The first assumption is that you know how to play poker and understand basic terminology like Big Blind, flop, 3-bet and shove. If you do not currently know how to play poker there is an abundance of free resources online available which you would be better off looking at first, before studying PKO specific strategy.

We also assume that you have a basic understanding of how multi table tournaments work. You will have played quite a few of them, you understand the prize structures, you know how the strategy changes at different stages of the tournament and generally appreciate how they are different to cash games. You should also know what a Progressive Knockout (PKO) tournament is. We will cover in depth the differences in approach between regular tournaments and PKOs, but you will already be aware that in a PKO every player has a bounty on their head and you win a percentage of it (usually 50%) with the rest of it going on your head, which you can only win if you win the whole tournament. You know that winning the bounty is an immediate prize on top of the regular payouts in the final 15-20% of finishing positions. You probably at least have a hunch that most people will take bigger risks in the early stages of a PKO tournament compared to a normal MTT in an attempt to win those bounties.

You should have at least a reasonable understanding of the concept of Independent Chip Model (ICM), the calculation used to understand the current real-money value of a chip stack during different stages of a tournament. ICM is particularly important on the money bubble of tournaments and at the final table where the pay jumps are significant. We also expect that your previous final table experience will have introduced you to the ways in which the poker played differs when the pay jump is significant. We deliberated over whether to include a complete guide to ICM and final table play, but we realised it was beyond the remit of this book. We do have chapters on how to adjust specifically to ICM heavy situations in a PKO but this book is written with the expectation that you understand how ICM impacts the late stages and final tables of tournaments.

You should have an understanding of the concept of equity as it relates to a poker hand. For example, it is well documented that most pocket pairs are close to 50/50 against two over cards, so they usually have equity of around 50%. Pocket Aces is a favourite against all hands and has more than 80% equity against most ranges. At the start of this book we have a lengthy section on some of the standard equity matchups common hands have against common ranges. Do not skip this section, it arguably renders the rest of the book useless if you do not have a solid understanding of preflop equity and how you need to adjust accordingly in PKOs.

The examples in this book will not be about how to play a specific hand in a specific spot, but instead will look at different situations and then determine what *range* of hands you would need to call, shove or fold. The importance of always thinking about your entire range is magnified in PKO format because the big decisions you make are often preflop. When we look at whether to call an all-in we will not be looking at it from the perspective of Ace King or Pocket Jacks, but the full selection of profitable calling hands, and, by inference, the full range of hands we would not call with.

With that in mind, when we talk about a range of hands for brevity we start with the weakest part of that range that qualifies. When we say an opponent's shoving range is:

AJs+, ATo+, KQs, 88+, A3o-A4o

That means:

AJ, AQ and AK suited

AT, AJ, AQ and AK offsuit
A3 and A4 offsuit
KQ suited
88, 99, TT, JJ, QQ, KK, AA

Are all part of that range.

Throughout this book we will be looking at different situations and analysing the profitability of every hand in your range. So rather than looking at how Ace King does against a shove from a tight player, we look at how every single hand would fare in that spot. It's not enough to know whether Ace King is a call or a fold, you need to know all the hands you would call and all the hands you would fold, so you are prepared for every situation. For this reason, we will sometimes present the table below with the equity of every hand.

The bottom left white boxes are unsuited hands (So in this table AK offsuit has 54% equity) and the top right grey boxes are suited hands (So AK suited has 56% equity). The darker grey boxes that run diagonally downwards across the table are pocket pairs (So here KK is the one with 71% equity).

	A	K	Q	J	T	9	8	7	6	5	4	3	2
A	85%	56%	50%	43%	37%	33%	33%	32%	31%	32%	32%	32%	31%
K	54%	71%	39%	38%	37%	36%	34%	34%	33%	33%	33%	33%	32%
Q	47%	36%	66%	38%	36%	36%	34%	32%	32%	32%	32%	31%	31%
J	40%	34%	34%	60%	36%	36%	34%	32%	31%	31%	31%	30%	30%
T	33%	33%	33%	33%	54%	36%	34%	33%	31%	30%	29%	29%	29%
9	30%	32%	32%	32%	32%	49%	35%	34%	32%	31%	30%	30%	29%
8	29%	31%	30%	30%	30%	32%	46%	34%	32%	31%	30%	29%	29%
7	28%	31%	29%	29%	29%	30%	30%	42%	33%	32%	30%	29%	27%
6	27%	30%	28%	27%	27%	28%	29%	29%	39%	32%	32%	29%	28%
5	29%	29%	28%	27%	26%	27%	28%	28%	28%	38%	32%	30%	29%
4	28%	29%	28%	27%	26%	26%	26%	26%	27%	28%	37%	30%	29%
3	28%	29%	27%	26%	25%	26%	25%	25%	26%	27%	27%	37%	28%
2	27%	28%	27%	26%	25%	35%	25%	24%	24%	25%	25%	25%	36%

You are not expected to memorise any of these specific ranges, nor should you come back to these tables expecting to find the precise answer to a hand you played. What we would like you to do is look at the inflection point within certain ranges, which hands become profitable, which ones do not, and the differences between them.

For example, you might notice above how quickly big Ace hands decrease in value: AKs has 56% equity here but A9s only has 33%.

However, the difference between Queen high hands is much narrower, QJs has 38% equity and Q2s has 32% equity. You may also, for example, notice that A6s is actually weaker than A5s which doesn't immediately make sense until you realise A5s can make a wheel straight and A6s cannot. We will make observations throughout the book but your focus when you look at these tables should be broadly on the range, not individual hands.

We have a general assumption that you are a serious amateur player rather than a professional. The advice in this book is aimed at both amateurs and professionals alike (in fact some of it we consider very advanced), but it is written mostly with amateurs in mind to make it accessible to both parties.

We have ordered the content in this book in terms of importance for your own PKO game, not in a linear way from the early stages to the middle, then the endgame. We start with some foundational material on equity against standard ranges, then we focus on calls, then ICM, then shoves, but our section on opening ranges is near the end. It might not make sense right away, but we believe you will get the most bang for your buck learning in this order.

We want to make it clear that this book is a guide to how to adjust from a normal MTT strategy to one where bounties are on the line. We will not be covering every stage of an MTT, different stack depths, different table positions or the complexities of post flop play in significant detail like a regular MTT book might. Instead we are looking at how the bounties impact common decisions so you can learn how to adapt your own game. Every piece of advice in this book is written with the bounties in mind.

Finally, we want to acknowledge that this is the first book written on PKOs and we don't think it will be the last. We expect the strategy advice to evolve and in particular the solver technology used for PKOs. Indeed, we found that the solver technology advanced while we were writing this book. We believe this book will stand the test of time as PKO strategy advances, but we expect our readers to continue their own study beyond this book to keep up with it.

With the obvious out of the way, let's dive in...

Chapter 1. Why play PKO's?

The fact you have bought this book means you have your own reasons for playing PKOs, but let's look at a few reasons you may have not considered.

The main reason to play PKOs is that they are enjoyable. The action is fast, there is more gambling involved, you can win money right away and winning a big bounty, or several bounties in one hand is a satisfying feeling. The reason why PKOs have gone from relative obscurity to the foundation of online poker room MTT schedules is, arguably, that PKOs are fun.

That brings us to the next reason to play PKOs and that is that recreational players enjoy them, which means they are soft. It gives them a chance to blow off steam and gamble, and as you will discover the common recreational player trait of playing too loose is forgiven a little in PKOs. PKOs give recreational players more winning moments, which creates a paradox for serious players in that their edge is lower but they are ultimately more profitable than normal MTTs because so many casual players are in the field.

The next reason, therefore, to play PKOs is that a lot of good MTT regulars avoid them because their edge is lower and there is too much gambling. A common mental game leak of otherwise good professional poker players is that they don't recognise when occasionally losing to a recreational is good for their profitability in the long term. The amateur player who wins now and then is going to come back for more, the player who gets crushed every time is going to find their entertainment elsewhere on Netflix or Fortnite. So PKOs are not only full of amateurs, the solid regulars are also much smaller in numbers too.

Maybe the biggest long term reason to play PKOs is that online poker operators like them, so they are going to figure more and more in their MTT schedules. The reason operators like them is because the prize pool gets spread around much more widely, so more players can play on their site for longer. In a normal MTT only 15-20% of the field gets a prize and that is usually the best players who withdraw it to their bank accounts. Given that most recreational players do not observe proper, or any, bankroll management guidelines this often means once they are out of the tournament they no longer have money on the site. In a PKO a much bigger percentage of the field gets a prize which they can use to continue to play on the site, which means more potential rake to be generated for the operator. PKOs really help an operator's ecosystem, they are not going anywhere.

Finally, and no doubt the reason you find yourself reading this book, there is currently a significant gap in the market for PKO strategy advice. They remain a relatively unsolved form of tournament poker and even the ICM calculators are only just catching up to them. A lot of professional poker players are unsure of how to adjust to them and often the correct play is something wildly different to what it would be in normal MTTs. Serious amateur players know the strategy is different but inevitably fall into the trap of playing too tight or too loose. One of the reasons we chose to write this book is because PKOs are as big a divergence from regular tournament strategy as the last topic we wrote about, satellites. Unlike satellites where a lot of the answers are clear cut and definitive, there are way more unknowns in PKOs.

PKOs are not going anywhere, so we may as well get started right now.

Chapter 2. PKO's in 30 minutes

To get the most out of this book we want to give you the foundations to review your own play away from the tables, so you develop a solid understanding of when to fight for bounties. We want the common scenarios to have come up so frequently in your self-study that you develop a solid instinct for some of the tricky spots this format conjures up.

We know this process will take some time. You are not expected to read a book in one sitting (in fact, you should make notes and return several times to important sections) neither are you expected *not* to play poker before you complete the book. We also appreciate that you may be reading this book literally before you play in a big PKO tournament later today. We want to fix the biggest leaks in your PKO game right away so you can see the important concepts working in practice before you get deep into the theory. We will explain the *why* behind these adjustments as you read this book. Until then, take our word for it and hopefully this chapter alone might improve your PKO game considerably.

The philosophy of PKOs

If you have read our previous book, *Poker Satellite Strategy,* it isn't the worst advice to say that in PKOs you should do the complete opposite of what you would do in a satellite. In satellites you make some extreme folds with strong hands because the prize structure is all or nothing, you don't get more for winning more chips. In a PKO you make some extreme calls with weak hands because the presence of bounties gives you an extra incentive to win a hand beyond increasing your chip stack.

Something which we will talk about a lot in this book is that there are two opposing forces in PKO tournaments that influence every decision we make. One force is the bounties themselves which are an immediate cash prize for eliminating another player. The other force is the Independent Chip Model (ICM) which is a way of determining the cash value of your chips in a tournament. Your chips are worth more or less at different stages of a tournament and often that means chip preservation is more important than winning more chips, so as such we play tighter than we would in a ChipEV spot such as a cash game.

A PKO is a constant battle between whether the bounty or ICM has a bigger influence on how you should play. Sometimes a bounty is so big that you should go for it with no care for what it will do to your chip stack if you lose. Sometimes the downside of losing when the payouts are substantial means you need to dial back your ranges and not let the bounty tempt you.

The purpose of this book is to give you the tools you need to determine in which spots you should be listening to the influence of the bounty and which spots you should be letting ICM have the final say. Until you have read this book completely, when you are at the tables try to think about what your normal range would be, then ask yourself if the bounty is enough to justify widening that range, or if ICM is pulling you in the other direction. Right now this process will be art rather than science, but it is a useful question to ask yourself every time you play a hand in a PKO.

Play looser when you can win a bounty

What makes PKOs radically different to normal MTTs is the presence of bounties. Winning a bounty not only is an immediate cash prize, it does the double-whammy and gives you a bigger stack to serve you as you try to win a payout and more bounties. The upside of getting all your money in the middle of the table when you can win a bounty is far greater than it is in a normal tournament where you just win chips.

For this reason, the equity you need to call a shove when you can win a bounty is lower than it would be in a regular ChipEV spot and much lower than it would be in an ICM influenced spot. In a scenario where you would need 50% equity to call in a cash game, you might need 60% equity to call in a tournament near the payouts, but in PKOs you might only need 35% equity. PKOs are a unique beast in that you often have to make a call that you know will lose you chips in the long term because the times you win the bounty more than make up for it.

For example, let's say you are playing in an $11 PKO and a player (whom you cover) shoves for 15 big blinds with a $30 bounty on their head. It's way before the money and the first mincash is $18. Without doing any calculations whatsoever, or thinking about your own chip stack, you can easily see that the bounty itself is worth more than the mincash. Not to mention if you win you will have a lot more chips to make the money and capture more bounties!

Don't worry about working out the maths yet, that's what this book is for. Until you have gone through all the material just take a look at how big the bounties are at your favourite site and think of them as removing a few percentage points from the equity you need to call. A small bounty might reduce the equity you need to call by 5%, a big bounty might reduce it by 12%. You might need ATo to call in a normal MTT but in the same spot in a PKO only need A8o, for example.

Again, it's art, not science, right now. The above advice is incredibly simplistic and only meant for your next few steps before you learn more about PKOs.

Pay attention to who covers whom at all times

This is a very important skill to make into a habit. If we assume that everyone is aware of the bounties on offer at the table, then knowing who can eliminate whom at any stage really shapes the ranges you can put them on. If, for example, a player opens under-the-gun with a medium stack with several players covering them, you can usually put them on a tight range because they risk elimination and will likely get called. However, if that same player opens and the Big Blind is a micro stack with a big bounty, you can widen their range because they are probably taking a punt at winning the Big Blind's bounty.

If nothing else, pay attention to who you can bust and who can bust you every single hand. You can widen your range accordingly when you have a chance at winning your bounty and likewise look at who appears to be trying to isolate you for your bounty.

Play more pots vs people you cover

When you can eliminate another player and win their bounty, the focus should be on how you can keep them in the pot for long enough that a chance to get all their chips comes up.

First and foremost, play more pots against them. That means defending your big blind wider than normal when they are in the pot and opening more hands when they are acting behind you. "You have to be in it to win it" is usually terrible poker advice, but it applies here.

This also means doing more things to keep them in pots, which often might mean giving them less chance to get away cheaply. For example, if a player who covers you opens, you are the Small Blind and the Big Blind has a bounty you can win, that might mean flatting with strong hands you would normally 3-bet. If you have Pocket Aces you might normally reraise to get the hands heads-up against the opener, but that gives the Big Blind an easy fold. If you just call you give them a good price to come along. Of course, you will get sucked out on more playing tricky, but the times you win the bounty more than makes up for it.

Play (close to) normal when you are covered

When you are the player who risks elimination in a hand and thus cannot win a bounty, that changes things considerably. There is no additional prize to win, you can only win chips, so as such you should not be taking big risks all-in. This does not mean you should be playing overly tight either because those chips are still worth winning as they are in a regular tournament.

If in doubt, just play the hand like it is a regular tournament without bounties, but with an adjustment for your opponents being quite loose-aggressive. Although you cannot win a bounty, there is one on your head to be won, so while you may be playing a regular MTT strategy, your opponents will be trying to get all your chips in the middle of the table. Treat it like you are playing a regular MTT against a table of maniacs where you expect to be called and reraised much more often. This does mean you can widen the range of hands you are prepared to value bet and bluff catch with, just not to the extent you would when you have a chance of winning a bounty.

Play to get the chips in

When you do have the potential to win a bounty and you have made a hand or massive draw, a cardinal sin of PKOs would be leaving chips on the table. If you get cute making small inducing bets in the hopes the bounty will reshove, you not only lose those extra chips when your strategy doesn't work out you also miss a bounty. Be prepared to bet big when you think you have a good enough hand to win a bounty. If you have a hand that could win a bounty make sure you, in the words of Doyle Brunson, "put your opponent to a decision for all their chips".

Fold equity is the least important form of equity in a PKO

Bluffing really isn't much of a thing in PKOs. Yes, there are spots and players where you can take down a pot knowing you have the worst hand, but as a general rule, you should play with the expectation that people are looking to call against you, especially when they can win a big bounty. When your bounty is big enough it will sometimes be correct for your opponents to call you with 100% of their range; don't complain if you try to steal a pot and it goes terribly, your opponent has a much bigger incentive to call you than usual.

That said, this doesn't mean you should be shoving and raising with a tight range, quite the opposite. Knowing that you will get called lighter than usual, you can sometimes shove wider correctly knowing you will get called by a lot of weaker hands that would never normally call you. Plus, now and then, you will take down the pot uncontested.

For this reason, you will have to adjust your shoving range to be weighted more towards hands that do well at showdown. Hands which don't need to improve against a wide range. Small pairs do worse in PKOs because they get called by a very wide range that is usually flipping against them. High broadway hands do better in PKOs than regular MTTs, not because they contain blockers, but because they get called by hands they dominate more often. Shoving from the cutoff with K3 suited might get a call from JT offsuit and hold, for example. This is something that you would never see in a regular tournament. We will explore in much more detail how different types of hands perform against different ranges in the next chapter.

The first time I ever played a bounty tournament was my second year as a professional. My best friend at the time, Rob Taylor, who was one of Ireland's top pros, was invited to the opening of a poker club and they gave him a free buy-in but put a big bounty on his head. He was asked to invite another pro along so he asked me. We were the only players with bounties on our head and the prize for busting us was about five buy-ins.

As we were driving there we were discussing how to play under these circumstances because we never had before. Rob was concerned that having the bounty on our head was so minus EV it was taking away the EV of the free buy-in. As the tournament progressed, Rob got more frustrated because he could not get any folds at all. I thought it wasn't a bad thing overall because when we do get a hand we might get paid.

I decided we had to accept a number of things; we had to accept that when we opened, we might get five calls, therefore we had to change our opening range. A hand like JTs becomes really good because it can make the nuts more often than other hands on boards that also give opponents big hands. My second adjustment was that clearly there was no point bluffing or semi-bluffing because you can't get folds. So in-game I changed my style to never bluff, value bet only and changed my sizings to bigger bets when I had it because they had to call me. Rob thought it was a handicap to have these bounties on our heads but it actually became a positive, it made the strategy simple, we just had to ask ourselves if our hands were really strong, would weaker hands call and then continue going with it?

This is why Phil Hellmuth still wins tournaments, because everybody wants to bust him. He complains about people calling him with shit but that is how he wins. When you have a bounty on your head, it turns you into Phil Hellmuth.

Key takeaways

- Play looser when you can win a bounty
- Play as if it's a normal MTT with some maniacs on the table when you are covered

- Don't leave chips on the table when you have a good enough hand to win a bounty
- Don't expect bluffs to work often
- High card hands hold up more often in PKOs than small pairs

Chapter 3. Standard ranges

Before we look at the calculations you need to make in PKOs we first must become familiar with what the most common standard ranges you will face are and which hands perform well against them in typical ChipEV situations. You need to know if Pocket Eights is a call or a fold in a non-PKO situation so that you can expand your ranges accordingly when a bounty is on the line.

Please don't skip this section, especially if you think you know these already. The rest of the book is predicated on you having a solid baseline understanding of the breakeven ranges you need in typical spots. By breakeven we mean knowing what the bottom of your range can be to get your money in the middle of the table and not lose money. For example if you need 44% equity to be breakeven and 77 and AJs are the weakest hands with that equity, everything below should be a fold. Once you identify the worst hand you can call with, you don't have to think about all the other hands. The tables we use in this book might seem complicated but really they are just about identifying what the bottom of your range should be as well as understanding how dramatically the hands change in value against different ranges.

How much equity you need to call a bet normally depends on the size of the bet you are facing. In PKOs this is going to be different because you are not just calling to win the chips but also the bounty. We will be explaining in more detail how to adjust for this but until then here is a handy guide about how much equity you need to call a bet profitably in a non-PKO, non-ICM pot.

To calculate the equity you need to call a bet, do the following calculation

How much it costs to call/final pot size when you do call *100

So if it costs you $5 to call a $5 bet into a pot with $2.50 already in the middle of the table, if you did call the final pot size would be $12.50, so that would be:

*$5/$12.50*100= 40%*

Below are some common bet sizes you might face and the equity you need to call (antes are excluded for simplicity):

Bet size	Equity Needed
100BB open shove when you are BB	49%
20BB 3-bet when you raised 2BB (Small vs Big Blind)	45%
10BB shove from Small Blind when you are Big Blind	44%
2x pot	40%
1.5x pot	37.50%
Pot size	33%
3/4 pot	30%
1/2 pot	25%
1/3 pot	20%
1/4 pot	16.5%

As you can see when the bet is small you don't need a big hand to call with at all because the risk to reward ratio is so great in your favour. However, when a player open shoves with a big stack your equity has to be much greater. Keep in mind in particular as we go through this chapter the hands where you need around 42-44% equity as that will be your breakeven equity for calling a 10 big blind push a lot of the time, and that is probably the most common preflop scenario you will face in MTTs.

Ideally, you will spend quite a bit of time on this section before moving to the next chapter, or at least return to it. You should also look online for an equity calculator, there are plenty of free ones available as well as in-built ones in software like *PokerTracker*. Here you can perform your own calculations about how particular hands perform against predetermined ranges. Don't worry about looking up the strength of every hand against that range like we have, just play around with hands that interest you.

The ranges we are using here are ones where we make an assumption about the player population in typical live and online tournaments. These are not Game Theory Optimal ranges. Again, this is why we implore you to study ranges away from this book based on your own assumptions of what a different player's opening ranges would be.

One more time before we get started, you are not expected to memorise any of these ranges or use them as definitive guides on how to play specific hands in any spot. The purpose is to look at where the breakeven points typically start and to observe the differences between hands within the ranges.

Against a tight range

Let's start by looking at how well different hands perform against what we would typically deem the 'Premium Hands' in poker, the top 9% of opening hands. This will obviously differ for different players, some might get rid of the smaller pairs in favour of hands that play well post flop like KQs, but for argument's sake we will say that a tight range looks like this:

AT+
66+

This is a good range to study because not only is it that which you would associate with a typical tight player, it is also not dissimilar to the typical range which might 3-bet your opening raise preflop.

Against that range, let's look at what hands perform well against it:

	A	K	Q	J	T	9	8	7	6	5	4	3	2
A	85%	56%	50%	43%	37%	33%	33%	32%	31%	32%	32%	32%	31%
K	54%	71%	39%	38%	37%	36%	34%	34%	33%	33%	33%	33%	32%
Q	47%	36%	66%	38%	36%	36%	34%	32%	32%	32%	32%	31%	31%
J	40%	34%	34%	60%	36%	36%	34%	32%	31%	31%	31%	30%	30%
T	33%	33%	33%	33%	54%	36%	34%	33%	31%	30%	29%	29%	29%
9	30%	32%	32%	32%	32%	49%	35%	34%	32%	31%	30%	30%	29%
8	29%	31%	30%	30%	30%	32%	46%	34%	32%	31%	30%	29%	29%
7	28%	31%	29%	29%	29%	30%	30%	42%	33%	32%	30%	29%	27%
6	27%	30%	28%	27%	27%	28%	29%	29%	39%	32%	32%	29%	28%
5	29%	29%	28%	27%	26%	27%	28%	28%	28%	38%	32%	30%	29%
4	28%	29%	28%	27%	26%	26%	26%	26%	27%	28%	37%	30%	29%
3	28%	29%	27%	26%	25%	26%	25%	25%	26%	27%	27%	37%	28%
2	27%	28%	27%	26%	25%	35%	25%	24%	24%	25%	25%	25%	36%

You probably won't be that surprised at the findings here. Pocket Nines are not even 50% against this range because they are flipping or dominated most of the time. Likewise Ace Queen has to be suited to be 50% because it will also be dominated by lots of combinations of Ace King, as well as QQ-AA. Then for the most part it is just simply a case of all the hands slowly getting weaker. Suitedness will add a few percentage points to most hands, especially the connected cards, because making a flush or straight is your best shot against big made hands. For that reason there is not much difference between QJs and 78s in terms of equity, in fact 78s does as well as QJo. This is still not a reason to get those hands in the middle of the table in a normal MTT or ChipEV situation if you suspect you are against a tight range like this, but it is useful to know if you are facing a bet where you are getting a good price to call that you would be better off with 98s than A2o.

Against a standard opening range

Now let's look at when an opponent opens up their range a little bit more to include above-average hands that figure to be good most of the time when it is folded to them. This expands the range to the top 20% of hands, which is roughly what you would expect the good regulars to be opening from a lot of positions. These are all still hands that hold up often enough and also container blockers making them profitable as a bluff.

A2s+
A4o+
KQo
KTs+
33+

This is a good range to study because it is a fair estimation of a lot of open shoves you will face in the latter stages of a tournament, so the hands where you will need roughly 42-44% equity (depending on antes and if you are a blind) to be breakeven.

	A	K	Q	J	T	9	8	7	6	5	4	3	2
A	86%	64%	60%	57%	53%	49%	46%	44%	42%	41%	40%	39%	39%
K	62%	73%	44%	42%	41%	39%	38%	37%	37%	36%	36%	35%	35%
Q	58%	41%	69%	42%	41%	39%	38%	36%	36%	36%	35%	34%	34%
J	54%	39%	39%	66%	42%	40%	39%	37%	36%	35%	34%	34%	34%
T	51%	38%	38%	39%	63%	41%	39%	38%	36%	35%	34%	34%	33%
9	47%	36%	36%	37%	38%	60%	40%	38%	37%	35%	33%	33%	33%
8	44%	34%	34%	35%	36%	36%	57%	39%	37%	36%	34%	33%	33%
7	41%	34%	33%	34%	34%	35%	35%	55%	38%	36%	34%	33%	32%
6	38%	33%	33%	32%	33%	33%	34%	34%	52%	37%	35%	34%	32%
5	38%	33%	32%	32%	31%	32%	32%	33%	33%	50%	36%	34%	33%
4	37%	32%	31%	30%	30%	30%	30%	31%	31%	32%	46%	33%	32%
3	36%	31%	31%	30%	30%	30%	29%	29%	30%	31%	30%	44%	32%
2	35%	31%	30%	30%	30%	29%	29%	28%	28%	29%	28%	28%	43%

It should be no surprise that more hands are profitable against this range. Most of the pocket pairs and bigger Aces are now breakeven if you need around 42-44% equity as you do in a lot of 10 big blind shove scenarios. In that respect KQs is a notable inflection point, it is just about breakeven while KQo is not. Beyond that the ranges follow on in much the same manner that the tight range does, just every hand performs slightly better.

Against a wide range

Then, of course, you will find yourself in encounters with Loose Aggressive (LAG) players who open a much wider range. This range really is player dependent, some would favour opening 78s over K2s, for example. However, here is a rough estimation of what a LAG might open, which in this case is 33% of hands and still quite high card heavy with connectedness.

A2+
K8o+
K2s+
Q8s+
Q9o+
JTo+
J9s+
22+

Understanding this range is important as you start to take these lessons into PKO tournaments where you are going to get action against a wide variety of hands because the bounties have made playing them more profitable.

	A	K	Q	J	T	9	8	7	6	5	4	3	2
A	86%	66%	63%	61%	59%	55%	53%	51%	49%	49%	48%	48%	47%
K	65%	77%	52%	51%	49%	46%	43%	42%	41%	41%	40%	39%	39%
Q	61%	50%	72%	46%	44%	41%	39%	38%	38%	37%	37%	36%	36%
J	59%	48%	43%	68%	43%	40%	39%	38%	37%	36%	36%	35%	34%
T	57%	46%	41%	39%	65%	41%	39%	38%	37%	36%	35%	35%	34%
9	53%	42%	38%	37%	37%	61%	40%	39%	38%	36%	35%	34%	33%
8	50%	40%	36%	35%	36%	36%	58%	40%	39%	37%	35%	34%	33%
7	48%	39%	35%	34%	35%	36%	36%	56%	39%	38%	36%	35%	33%
6	46%	38%	34%	33%	34%	34%	35%	36%	54%	39%	37%	35%	34%
5	46%	37%	34%	33%	32%	33%	33%	34%	35%	52%	38%	36%	35%
4	45%	37%	33%	32%	32%	31%	32%	33%	34%	34%	52%	36%	34%
3	45%	36%	33%	31%	31%	30%	30%	31%	32%	33%	32%	48%	33%
2	44%	35%	32%	31%	30%	30%	30%	29%	30%	31%	30%	29%	45%

Against a wide range you can usually safely assume that all pairs and Aces are breakeven or better in a typical shoved pot. You can also put the better broadway hands in the middle of the table against a LAG open. For the most part pairs, Aces and big Kings are playable against a wide opener.

Against a Small Blind shove

This is probably the most common matchup you will face in any poker situation, which is when you are the Big Blind and it folds around to the Small Blind. It is very profitable for the Small Blind to shove a lot of hands, and also profitable to defend against them with a similarly wide range. In a tournament you are probably going to face the most short stack shoves from the Small Blind so it is very useful to know which hands have around 42-44% equity against a Small Blind shove.

A typical range for the Small Blind would be anything either connected or with an ounce of high card showdown value, so we think 49% of hands would be about right and look like this:

22+,
A2+
K2s+
K8o+
Q4s+
Q8o+
J6s+
J8o+
T6s+
T8o+
95s+
98o+
84s+
87o
74s+
76o
63s+

53s+
43s

	A	K	Q	J	T	9	8	7	6	5	4	3	2
A	84%	66%	64%	62%	61%	58%	57%	55%	53%	53%	52%	51%	51%
K	64%	78%	57%	56%	54%	52%	50%	49%	48%	47%	46%	46%	45%
Q	62%	55%	75%	53%	52%	49%	47%	45%	45%	44%	43%	42%	42%
J	60%	53%	50%	72%	50%	47%	45%	43%	42%	42%	41%	40%	40%
T	59%	52%	49%	47%	69%	46%	44%	43%	41%	40%	39%	39%	38%
9	56%	49%	46%	44%	43%	65%	43%	42%	41%	39%	38%	37%	37%
8	55%	47%	44%	42%	41%	40%	62%	42%	40%	39%	37%	36%	35%
7	52%	46%	42%	40%	39%	39%	38%	58%	40%	39%	37%	36%	35%
6	51%	45%	41%	39%	38%	37%	37%	37%	56%	39%	38%	36%	35%
5	50%	44%	41%	38%	36%	36%	35%	36%	36%	53%	38%	37%	35%
4	49%	43%	40%	38%	36%	34%	33%	34%	34%	35%	51%	36%	35%
3	48%	42%	39%	37%	35%	34%	32%	32%	33%	34%	33%	49%	34%
2	48%	42%	39%	36%	35%	33%	31%	31%	31%	31%	31%	31%	47%

We will jump right into the next example which is very similar for our analysis, we just wanted to highlight Small Blind vs Big Blind ranges because they come up so often.

Against any two cards

It's very important to know how your hand holds up against any two cards or a 'random hand' as there are a lot of situations where you will be up against a range of 100%. Sometimes a player can shove 100% of their hands because it is unexploitable, some do it to abuse tight players or ICM, some players are predictable and others are just maniacs. In PKOs, especially when your bounty is big, don't be surprised to see players do anything to try and win it.

	A	K	Q	J	T	9	8	7	6	5	4	3	2
A	85%	67%	66%	65%	65%	63%	62%	61%	60%	60%	59%	58%	57%
K	65%	82%	64%	63%	62%	60%	58%	58%	57%	56%	55%	54%	53%
Q	64%	61%	80%	60%	59%	58%	56%	54%	54%	53%	52%	51%	50%
J	64%	61%	58%	77%	58%	56%	54%	52%	51%	50%	49%	48%	47%
T	63%	60%	57%	55%	75%	54%	52%	51%	49%	47%	47%	46%	45%
9	61%	58%	55%	53%	51%	72%	51%	49%	47%	46%	44%	43%	42%
8	60%	56%	54%	51%	50%	48%	69%	48%	46%	45%	43%	41%	40%
7	59%	55%	52%	50%	48%	46%	45%	66%	45%	44%	42%	40%	38%
6	58%	54%	51%	48%	46%	44%	43%	42%	63%	43%	41%	40%	38%
5	58%	53%	50%	47%	44%	43%	41%	41%	40%	60%	41%	40%	38%
4	57%	52%	49%	46%	44%	41%	39%	39%	38%	38%	57%	37%	37%
3	56%	51%	48%	45%	43%	40%	37%	37%	36%	36%	35%	54%	36%
2	55%	51%	47%	44%	42%	39%	37%	35%	34%	34%	33%	32%	50%

It is no surprise to see that when our opponent's range gets wider, the number of hands that become profitable to call with does too. There are a couple of interesting nuggets of information that are worth gleaning from a closer inspection here. First of all, if you compare these ranges to the first two quite tight ranges at the start of this chapter, you will see that against a completely random range a hand like Pocket Eights performs much better than Ace King, however against a tight range Ace King performs better than Pocket Eights. The reason for this switch around is because when the ranges are narrow you are up against pairs and Ace high hands, so spiking an Ace or King is often needed to win. Plus, when you have an Ace and a King yourself, it is less likely your opponent has one. However, when it could be any two cards you are facing, a hand like Pocket Eights tends to hold its own because it doesn't need to improve to win. That is really worth knowing if you suspect your opponent is pushing with anything. It's also worth knowing for our own shoving ranges if we are expecting to get called wide.

The bigger lesson, one which you should internalise for PKOs as this is going to come up later, is that when you are up against a wide range, high card hands go up in value. Against tighter ranges the Ace high hands decrease in value quite quickly, for example against a standard range AKs has 64% equity and A2s has 39%, so 25% difference. Against any two cards AKs has 67% equity and A2s has 57%, a difference of just 10%. The other Broadway hands also perform very well with a much narrower decrease in strength between hands. The reason for this is not the effect of card removal, as some may suspect, but because against a wide range these hands tend to win at showdown without having to improve. KJs might actually be the best hand on the river (even if it completely misses) when your opponent is closing their eyes and shoving without looking.

It's worth repeating to give you a head start for the next sections - when the ranges are wide, high cards go up in value.

Against a capped opening range

We are heading into more complex range construction now but some players will shove their strong hands but cannot bring themselves to do it when they have a monster like AA–QQ, so rather than shove they will min raise with those hands to try and induce action. This tends to happen in shallow stack situations and in big fields where balancing your range is not as important. A capped opening range of shoves would probably look like this:

A2s+
A4o+
KQo
KTs+
33–JJ

Again, because by definition these bets tend to be shoves, look for the hands which have roughly 42–44% equity against them for your breakeven point.

	A	K	Q	J	T	9	8	7	6	5	4	3	2
A	87%	65%	62%	59%	55%	51%	48%	45%	42%	42%	40%	40%	39%
K	64%	74%	45%	43%	42%	40%	38%	38%	38%	37%	36%	36%	35%
Q	60%	42%	72%	43%	43%	41%	39%	38%	38%	37%	36%	36%	35%
J	57%	40%	40%	69%	44%	42%	40%	39%	37%	37%	36%	36%	35%
T	53%	39%	40%	41%	67%	42%	41%	39%	38%	36%	35%	35%	35%
9	48%	37%	38%	39%	39%	63%	41%	40%	38%	36%	35%	35%	34%
8	45%	35%	36%	37%	38%	38%	60%	40%	39%	37%	35%	34%	34%
7	42%	35%	34%	35%	36%	36%	37%	67%	39%	37%	35%	34%	33%
6	39%	34%	34%	34%	34%	35%	35%	36%	55%	38%	36%	35%	33%
5	39%	33%	33%	33%	33%	33%	33%	34%	34%	52%	37%	35%	34%
4	37%	32%	32%	32%	32%	31%	31%	32%	32%	33%	49%	34%	33%
3	36%	32%	32%	32%	32%	31%	30%	30%	31%	32%	31%	46%	33%
2	36%	32%	32%	32%	31%	31%	30%	29%	30%	30%	29%	29%	44%

Against two opponents

How your hand holds up against two players is very important to know in PKOs. It happens much less in regular MTTs and when it does you can assume at least the 2nd player in the pot has a very strong hand. That is not the case in PKOs where the only thing better than winning one bounty is winning two. You really need to know equity against two opponents in PKOs. In this example we have assumed both opponents have a standard 20% opening range from the previous example but in your self-study you can certainly experiment widening those ranges or indeed by adding more opponents.

	A	K	Q	J	T	9	8	7	6	5	4	3	2
A	67%	39%	36%	34%	32%	29%	27%	25%	24%	24%	22%	22%	21%
K	36%	60%	37%	34%	33%	31%	29%	28%	27%	26%	25%	25%	24%
Q	33%	33%	54%	35%	34%	31%	29%	27%	26%	26%	25%	24%	24%
J	31%	31%	31%	49%	33%	30%	28%	27%	25%	24%	23%	23%	23%
T	29%	30%	30%	30%	45%	30%	29%	27%	25%	23%	22%	22%	22%
9	26%	27%	27%	27%	28%	40%	28%	27%	25%	23%	21%	21%	20%
8	25%	25%	25%	26%	26%	26%	37%	27%	25%	23%	21%	20%	20%
7	23%	24%	23%	24%	24%	25%	25%	34%	26%	24%	22%	20%	19%
6	21%	24%	23%	22%	23%	23%	24%	24%	32%	25%	23%	21%	20%
5	21%	23%	22%	22%	20%	21%	22%	22%	23%	29%	23%	21%	20%
4	20%	23%	21%	21%	20%	19%	20%	20%	21%	21%	26%	20%	19%
3	18%	21%	20%	20%	19%	19%	18%	18%	19%	20%	19%	25%	18%
2	18%	20%	20%	20%	19%	18%	18%	17%	17%	18%	17%	16%	24%

The immediate thing to notice is how all the hands go down quite significantly in value, for the obvious reason that with two opponents you are going to win less frequently even with a monster like Pocket Aces. Do remember, however, that in a three-way pot that doesn't make the hands necessarily less profitable, because more money is in the pot and thus we get a better return when we do win. We usually need much less equity to call in a multiway pot in a ChipEV/non-ICM heavy hand. For example, if we are the Big Blind and two players have pushed all-in for 10 big blinds each ahead of us, we only usually need 30% equity to break even (*$9/$30*100= 30%*). So while AQs has gone from 60% equity against one standard range to 36% against two players with standard ranges, it still would be profitable to call against two small stack shoves.

The more interesting thing to note here, and this is particularly important to understand before we move onto PKOs, is how certain hands go up in value relative to others. For example, notice that some of the King high hands are stronger than their Ace high equivalent. KQs has 37% equity and AQs has just 36%. KTs has 33% equity compared to ATs with 32%. Even lesser broadway hands like QTs and JTs outperform ATs. The same is true for the offsuit hands. Why is this?

The reason is that when you are putting your money in the middle of the table against multiple opponents, if you don't have a monster you want to have a *live* hand. That is a hand where if you hit you are not worried about being dominated. 67s performs quite well against ATo, for example, in no small part because it hits more straights and flushes. When it hits its pair, two pair, set and full house hands it is less likely to be outkicked. When ATo hits top pair it is often up against a better Ace or there is potential for to be up against a broadway-type of straight. If you hit, for example, two pair with 67 you usually are not worried about anyone else having a 6 or a 7.

This is not to say it's favourable to have the weaker but live hand, of course you would still prefer to have ATo rather than 67s in this spot. However it is valuable to learn that hands which are not profitable in heads-up pots can become profitable with multiple opponents when the ROI is generous and they are likely to be very live.

You'll notice that the medium to low pocket pairs do not decrease in value at the same rate as the big Ace type hands. They occupy an interesting middle ground where they sometimes might hold against two cards without improvement but also can spike a set to win with a monster.

Once again, you are not expected to memorise these ranges, just observe how they differ from each other in different scenarios. Download one of the many free poker equity calculators out there and play around with your own examples. When you feel comfortable that you have a baseline knowledge of how ranges get stronger or weaker based on our opponent tendencies, it is time to look at how we adjust for Progressive Knockout Tournaments.

Key takeaways

- Whether a hand is profitable depends on how much equity we have against a range and how much it costs to call a bet
- Having 42% equity is usually break even when our opponent shoves for 10 big blinds
- High cards go up in value when our opponent's range is wide
- Live hands go up in value in multiway pots

Chapter 4. How the bounty changes everything

At the start of a normal MTT (assuming equal skill) your equity is the buy-in excluding the rake. If you play a $215 online MTT ($200 + $15) and you are an average skilled player your stack is worth $200 at the start of the tournament. Our equity is the sum of winning each prize in the tournament. In a 100 runner field the chance of winning each prize is 1%. You have a 1% chance of coming 1st, a 1% chance of coming 2nd and a 1% chance of coming 100th.

In a satellite your equity is the same. In a $215 satellite your equity is still $200 after rake and in a 100 runner field the chance of winning each prize is 1%. The difference between satellites and normal MTTs is the prizes are all the same, 1st might get the same as 10th, for example.

In a PKO your equity at the exact start of the tournament is the same, in a $215 PKO your equity is $200. Where PKOs are different from normal MTTs and satellites is that rather than equity just being our chance of winning each prize, it is also our chance of winning each bounty. This is a really important concept to understand in PKOs so we will repeat:

In a PKO our equity is the sum of all our chances of winning each prize PLUS our chance of winning each bounty.

The prize pool is split between the payouts and the reward for busting each opponent. In a 100 runner field the chance of finishing in each position is the same, 1%. The chance of winning each bounty is also 1%.

Let's look at how that changes the way we play a PKO compared to normal tournaments. We are using a simplified example each time with just 10 players but the principles you are about to see remain true whether it's 10, 100 or 1,000 players in the tournament. This hypothetical example is also from a $215 tournament. Regardless of the format, our equity at the start after rake is $200. This example is a ten-person MTT with a $215 buy-in, a 10,000 starting stack and three players get paid. $1,000 for 1st, $600 for 2nd and $400 for first.

MTT
Players: 10
Buy-in: $200 + $15
Starting Stack: 10,000
Payouts: $1,000/$600/$400

Now imagine if two players went all-in the first hand, the loser's equity goes down to $0 for the obvious reason they are no longer in the tournament, but how much equity does the winner gain?

If you have read our previous book, you will know the answer is not an additional $200. If you plug this into an ICM calculator you will discover the winner actually gains $168.89 of equity, making their new equity $368.89. So the question is, where does the remaining $31.11 go? The answer is it goes to the remaining eight players, who gain $3.89 in equity each. By virtue of the fact that they have all moved one step closer to the money without doing anything, their equity has increased. In this example the winner gains $168.89 for a risked loss of $200, which is why it would be a very bad idea to get all your money in early on a coinflip in a tournament. The breakeven equity required to call an all-in in this example would be 54.2%, not 50% as it would be in a cash game. This is why in most cases we play tighter in tournaments than in cash games, as we usually stand to lose more than we gain.

Start of $200+$15 MTT			
Payout	*Prize*	*Stack*	*Equity*
1st	$1,000	10,000	$200
2nd	$600	10,000	$200
3rd	$400	10,000	$200
4th		10,000	$200
5th		10,000	$200
6th		10,000	$200
7th		10,000	$200
8th		10,000	$200
9th		10,000	$200
10th		10,000	$200

After Two Players Get It All-in Hand #1			
Payout	*Prize*	*Stack*	*Equity*
1st	$1,000	20,000	$368.89
2nd	$600	10,000	$203.89
3rd	$400	10,000	$203.89
4th		10,000	$203.89
5th		10,000	$203.89
6th		10,000	$203.89
7th		10,000	$203.89
8th		10,000	$203.89
9th		10,000	$203.89
10th		0	$0

Before we compare that to a PKO tournament let's look at how this differs in a satellite situation because it provides some useful context for the rest of this discussion. Let's use the same criteria of a $215 tournament with ten players and 10,000 starting stacks, but instead we have four prizes of $500 satellite tickets each.

Satellite
Players: 10
Buy-in: $200 + $15
Starting Stack: 10,000
Payouts: $500/$500/$500/$500

Our equity at the start is once again $200 but what happens this time when two players get all-in against each other in the first hand?

This time around the winner gains $133.33 in equity (so they now have $333.33). This is dramatically lower than in the normal tournament example and even more so if it were just a cash game. $66.67 has disappeared and been redistributed between the other eight players ($8.33 each). This is why it is particularly important to play much tighter in satellites. In this example the winner gains $133.33 for a risked loss of $200, so the breakeven equity they require to get all-in is 60%. You need to be a very strong favourite to justify an early exit in a satellite.

Start of $200+$15 Satellite			
Payout	*Prize*	*Stack*	*Equity*
1st	$500	10,000	$200
2nd	$500	10,000	$200
3rd	$500	10,000	$200
4th	$500	10,000	$200
5th		10,000	$200
6th		10,000	$200
7th		10,000	$200
8th		10,000	$200
9th		10,000	$200
10th		10,000	$200

After Two Players Get It All-in Hand #1			
Payout	*Prize*	*Stack*	*Equity*
1st	$500	20,000	$333.33
2nd	$500	10,000	$208.33
3rd	$500	10,000	$208.33
4th	$500	10,000	$208.33
5th		10,000	$208.33
6th		10,000	$208.33
7th		10,000	$208.33
8th		10,000	$208.33
9th		10,000	$208.33
10th		0	$0

In a cash game when we double our stack we double our equity because there is a 1:1 correlation between chips and dollars. In a tournament that is not the case, which is why it is correct to play tighter, pot control, avoid flips and generally lower variance in tournaments. Even more so in satellites. So what changes when we are playing a PKO?

Using the same $215 example with ten players and 10,000 starting stacks, but it's a PKO so $100 goes into the normal prize pool and $100 into the bounty prize pool ($50 paid immediately when a player busts, $50 going on the head of the player who busts them). So if you bust a player in the first hand you win $50 and your own bounty becomes $100.

PKO
Players: 10
Buy-in: $200 + $15
Starting Stack: 10,000
Payouts: $500/$300/$200
Progressive Bounty: $100 ($50 paid immediately, $50 added to player bounty)

One more time, what happens when two players go all-in on the first hand? The loser's equity is $0, but what does the winner gain?

They actually gain $224.45. Their new total equity becomes $424.45.

How is this possible when only $400 of equity went into the middle of the table?

The reason is because they first win prize pool equity of $84.45, so their new equity for the payouts becomes $184.45.

Then they win the bounty itself, which is an immediate $50.

Then they win a bigger share of their own bounty, which in this case is worth $30.

Finally, they win an increased share of the other eight bounties at the table, in this case that is worth $160 ($20 for each player). By doubling our stack we effectively double the chance of winning each remaining bounty.

So in this example, the all-in winner gains $224.45 in equity for a risked loss of $200. A PKO is the only type of tournament where the potential gain is often greater than the loss when you go all-in. In this example the breakeven equity needed to get all-in is actually 47.1%. That means it can be mathematically correct to get your money in as an underdog because the upside, when you do win, outweighs the downside when you lose.

Comparing these examples to a cash game, the breakeven equity required to get all-in before you factor the final pot size is as follows:

Cash game: 50%
MTT: 54.2%
Satellite: 60%
PKO: 47.1%

Let's unpack what is happening in PKOs to dramatically change equities in tournaments. First of all, winning the bounty itself makes a big difference because it's an immediate payout. Once you win that it is removed from the prize pool, the other players cannot win it.

What is also happening when we win that early all-in is we are increasing our ability to win future bounties. Our chances of winning our own increased bounty (which is what happens when we win the entire tournament) have doubled to be worth $30 and our chances of winning the bounty of everyone else has also doubled from $10 to $20 per player. Because we have the chip lead there isn't a player at the table we cannot eliminate and for that reason we are the favourite to scoop up all the bounties.

When we cover our opponent we are competing for four different kinds of equity:

- The payouts
- An immediate bounty
- Our own bounty
- The bounties of the other players

So where does this additional equity come from? It comes from the other players at the table. Just as they gain equity in a normal MTT by sitting on the sidelines when two players get all-in, they lose equity when it happens in a PKO. In this example each player loses $3.06 of equity when they folded, because there is a $50 bounty they are never going to win because it has already been claimed. We'll expand on this shortly but this is why it's never a good idea to late register or rebuy in a PKO, because once the first player has been eliminated money has been taken from the prize pool. If somebody late registered in this hypothetical example they would immediately be down $3.06 of equity.

Start of $200+$15 PKO			
Payout	*Prize*	*Stack*	*Combined Equity*
1st	$500	10,000	$200
2nd	$300	10,000	$200
3rd	$200	10,000	$200
4th		10,000	$200
5th		10,000	$200
6th		10,000	$200
7th		10,000	$200
8th		10,000	$200
9th		10,000	$200
10th		10,000	$200

After Two Players Get It All-in Hand #1			
Payout	*Prize*	*Stack*	*Combined Equity*
1st	$500	20,000	$424.45 (including $50 already realised)
2nd	$300	10,000	$196.94
3rd	$200	10,000	$196.94
4th		10,000	$196.94
5th		10,000	$196.94
6th		10,000	$196.94
7th		10,000	$196.94
8th		10,000	$196.94
9th		10,000	$196.94
10th		0	$0

If two players get it in first hand they only need 47.1% equity against each other for it to be profitable. For that reason, it would actually be an advantage for two players to go all-in against each other blind on the first hand. In a normal tournament we would be hurting ourselves because the guy who wins does not double his equity, but in the PKO scenario he more than doubles it. It would actually be collusion to tell each other to do that, so please don't, but it's an example of how PKO strategy is really upside down compared to regular MTTs. The same is true in satellites, there are a lot of spots in satellites where one player can go all-in with 100% of their hands and their opponent should fold 100% of their hands because the ICM pressure is so extreme. Both ends of what we call the 'ICM dial', with satellites at one end and PKOs at the other, produce situations so extreme that both players could make the optimal decision without looking at their cards.

To further illustrate how the equities in a PKO dramatically change compared to the other formats you are used to, let's look at what happens after the first player has been eliminated. What happens when the chip leader goes looking for their next bounty? What happens when two shorter stacks go up against each other?

Chip leader vs short stack

It is the very next hand and the chip leader managed to get their chips in the middle of the table against a short stack (not really a short stack, they have the same chips as everyone else, but it's useful in PKOs to frame it this way because it's a quick way of identifying who can win the bounty in the hand and who cannot). A reminder that the chip leader has $374.45 of equity remaining in this tournament (after realising $50 of a bounty) and the short stack has $196.94.

If the short stack player wins the all-in, the equities flip. Shorty will now have 20,000 chips and $374.45 of equity and the former chip leader now has 10,000 chips and $196.94 of equity. We calculate breakeven equity by dividing the equity we lose when we bust by the equity we gain when we win so in this case 196.94/374.45 = 52.6%. So the short stack needs equity of 52.6% to justify getting their chips in the middle of the table. This is close to the 54.2% equity needed in the first example of a normal MTT which we explored at the start of this chapter. This perhaps makes intuitive sense why, because the short stack cannot win a bounty their decision is very close to what it would be in a normal tournament. When you are covered in a PKO you will always need more equity than in a cash game to call an all-in, just like in a regular tournament.

Looking at the same situation from the chip leader's perspective is very different. If the chip leader gets their money in against the short stack and wins, their new equity becomes $575, which again is more than the combined current equities ($571.39) of the two players. Again, let's unpack why. When the chip leader wins, they gain:

- ICM prize pool equity of $255
- Immediate bounty of $50
- Equity of winning future bounties including their own of $270

So the chip leader is gaining $200.55 but only potentially risking $177.51, so again the leader wins more than they risk. In this case 177/51/378.05 = 47% breakeven equity required to call. Once again 47% is the required equity to call in a PKO, meaning that it will be correct for the chip leader to get their money as an underdog but the shorter stack has to be much tighter.

Short stack vs short stack

Let's look at a second hypothetical example this time instead of the chip leader vs a short stack, what happens when it is a short stack vs a short stack? Once again, this is the second hand of the PKO after the first player has bust, but the chip leader has folded and two other players get their chips in the middle of the table. They both start the hand with exactly $196.94 at the start of the hand which one of them will lose, but what does the winner gain? The answer is they win an additional 222.86, taking their total equity up to 419.80.

This is broken down as follows:

- ICM prize pool equity of $87.86
- Immediate bounty of $50
- Equity of winning future bounties including their own of $85

They stand to win $222.86 for a risked loss of $196.94, so they stand to win more than they lose, meaning their breakeven equity in this spot is 46.9%. Very close to 47% as per the two previous examples. In this example it is correct for both players, because they have equal stacks and can both win the bounty, to get it in with less than 50% equity.

You are not expected to memorise the above or work out similar calculations on the fly, we will be covering the best way to do that in the following chapters. The above should help you understand the paradigm shift that is PKO strategy compared to regular MTTs. With that in mind, let's look at the broad ways in which this should change your overall strategy before jumping into how to calculate the right decisions in very complex scenarios.

Late registering and re-entering in PKOs

If it wasn't clear already, late registering or re-entering a PKO is always a bad idea. Every elimination sees at least 25% of a buy-in removed from the prize pool and the later you register, the smaller the prize pool you are playing for. Think of that 25% of a buy-in as an additional rake you have to pay. In a 100 runner $215 PKO, every player eliminated is like an extra $0.50 in rake you have to pay (the $50 bounty divided by 100 players). This isn't so bad if you late register near the start of the tournament where only a few players have bust, but terrible if you register at the last minute.

Late registering after five people bust a $215 PKO with 100 runners is not so bad, that's just an additional rake of $2.50 (five players bust worth $0.50 of rake each). Late registering that same PKO just before registration ends and 100 players have been eliminated is much worse, that is like adding at least an extra $10 rake before you even start. Because of the gambley nature of PKOs you can also expect a lot more eliminations than usual at the start, so if you can't register in the first 15 minutes of the tournament it's probably not worth it.

To frame it a different way, if you register on time for a PKO you actually gain equity from all the players who are going to register late. Your $200 of equity at the start of a $215 PKO is actually going to be worth a little more than $200. Just as there are implied odds when you play a speculative hand, there is implied equity when you early register a PKO. Trying to calculate such implied equity would be near impossible, so let's just say you are always better off registering on time, especially in PKOs with a long late registration period.

A lot of players seem to think late registering is good because the stacks have moved around a bit and some big bounties are out there. It's a cognitive dissonance because the bounties are bigger than at the start, so it seems like a better time to go in. The flaw is that these players are looking at the individual bounties, they are not looking at the total bounty pool. The sites are smart about this because they do not make it obvious how much of the bounty prize pool has gone. At the World Series of Poker Main Event final table they put all the millions of dollars on the table to show what is being played for, if they did that at the start of a PKO with all the money on a separate table and every time somebody won a bounty they got up and took their bounty from the table, people would soon realise how bad late registering is.

Early game strategy

In the early stages of a PKO the bounties are big relative to our equity, if you knock somebody out early in a PKO the bounty is worth roughly a third of a buy-in in equity. Early game strategy should be about maximising our chances of winning bounties from other players. You'll see players over adjust in each direction in PKOs, but the bigger mistake would be playing too tight in the early stages.

When we are the player who covers our opponents we need less than 50% breakeven equity to get all-in. When we are the player who is covered we need more than 50%, just like in a regular MTT. Therefore a big adjustment in PKOs is to play more hands against the players we cover while avoiding the players who can eliminate us. Whenever you play against somebody you cover you are playing for more equity than they are, so you can profitably get your money in lighter than they can.

You should focus on keeping players you cover in the hand, rather than taking down a pot preflop or with a continuation bet. This might include making small enticing raises, inducing bets that could be bluffed over or even limping/calling. If your normal strategy is to raise x3 on the Button but you cover both the Blinds and they fold you have no chance of winning their bounty. A smaller bet or even a limp is much more likely to get action.

An implication of that is you will play more multiway pots in PKOs. When the bet sizings are small and juicy bounties are on the line, more people are incentivised to play with speculative hands. Generally speaking it is good for you as one of the bigger stacks if more players call behind you because that is more bounties you can win.

In the early stages you should focus more on hands that play well multiway, which are usually suited Aces, suited and/or connected hands and small pairs. The hands that tend to flop the nuts, massive draws or completely miss. Avoid dominated hands that don't play well multiway like offsuit rag Aces and weak Broadway hands. With these hands you are much better narrowing the field by raising big or 3-betting to get the hand heads-up against one player.

Pay attention to the players that over adjust for bounties. We know you can get it in much wider in a PKO but some players go nuts and call a 100 big blind shove with Q7o. Identify who these players are and shove for value preflop with your big hands when they cover you, because you are much more likely to get looked up wide. It might seem insane to shove 100 big blinds preflop with Queens because in a regular MTT you are only going to get called by Aces or Kings, but in a PKO you can easily get called by a hand you completely dominate.

Midgame strategy

By the time we get to the middle stages the stacks will begin to vary significantly but more importantly the bounties will too. Some players will still be on their starting bounties but there will also be some very juicy ones out there, some even bigger than the original buy-in. We will still be a fair distance from the money so we still want to be targeting big bounties that we cover. Imagine if the biggest bounty on your table in a $215 PKO is short stacked, they have a $125 bounty and just ten big blinds. We would want to loosen up our opening range when that player is in the blinds, in some positions we might want to open any two cards.

In general there should be fewer multiway pots in the middle stages because the stacks are much shallower. For this reason, high card hands go up in value while the small pairs and suited connectors go down in value.

When you have a big bounty on your own head and a short stack, a mistake people make in this spot is to tighten their range because they expect to get called more often. This should not change how often you shove but it should change the range, again which should be weighted towards high cards. If you are going to get snapped called when you shove by any two cards, shoving a hand like 67s is bad because you are always getting called and are never ahead, but shoving a hand like K9o is actually profitable because you are often going to get called by much worse. Don't be surprised to shove a hand like KJo or QTs, get called and win the pot without improving in PKOs. In the middle stages when stacks are shallow but bounties are big, the main adjustment to your range should be weighting your range to high card hands with showdown value.

Endgame strategy

We are going to cover how to play PKOs when payouts are a more immediate factor in another chapter but we want to prime you ahead of that. The bounties are going to vary wildly at this stage and you will often find yourself in decisions involving bounties that are comparable in size to the next pay jump. ICM becomes a bigger factor and it will invariably contract your ranges in a similar way to how the bounty has expanded them.

In general the chip leader should play even looser than in a normal MTT endgame scenario. The chip leader covers everybody and in a lot of spots is the only person who can win some of these very big bounties. The chip leader can often open any two cards, especially in final table situations, because the prospect of taking a stand against them means not only risking missing a massive pay jump but also the big bounties. There is a lot of equity you risk missing when you take on the chip leader.

Short stacks have to play tighter than usual because they are going to get called light, so going out with a weak hand is a bad idea when the payouts are significant. Middle stacks should be bounty hunting the players they cover more aggressively because the upside of winning is huge at this stage, the bounties are often big and busting a player can often move them to the next pay jump.

Key takeaways

- In a PKO your upside is often greater than your downside when you go all-in, so you can actually call wider than in regular tournaments or ChipEV spots
- When you cover your opponent you are competing for four different kinds of equity - the payouts, the immediate bounty, your own bounty and future bounties of other players
- Late registering and re-entering PKOs is a bad idea because you cannot win the bounties already won

Chapter 5. Calculating calling ranges at the table

PKOs present some of the most complicated equity and ICM decisions you are likely to see in poker tournaments, which should be reassuring because it means as a format it is unlikely to ever be truly solved. We recommend you study individual spots away from the table using software like Holdem Resources Calculator and ICMZER. The more work you do away from the table, the easier these decisions will be in the moment. However, you also need a heuristic for working out equity adjustments in real time.

Before we get started on this, if you have skipped the chapter on equities against standard ranges, please revisit it now. It may seem like something you can ignore but having a foundational understanding of how hands perform against different ranges will make the adjustments you make that much easier in the moment.

We have developed a shorthand way to get a rough idea of how big the bounty and bet size should adjust your calling ranges in a PKO, which we call Bounty Factor.

Bounty Factor looks at the player you cover and divides their number of starting bounties by their number of starting stacks.

Starting Bounties/Starting Stacks

Different poker sites have different ways to express bounties. Some display the overall bounty but you only win half immediately and the other half goes on your head. In a $215 PKO it might show a $100 bounty but if you knock the player out you only win $50. Others display the actual cash amount you stand to win right away. In a $215 PKO it simply shows $50 and that is what you win. This doesn't matter for the purposes of working out Bounty Factor, it is the same calculation.

At the start of a tournament Bounty Factor for every player will always be 1 (1 starting stack/1 starting bounty).

To give an example in a $215 PKO with 10,000 starting stacks, your opponent whom you cover may have 20,000 chips and $300 which is three starting bounties, so 3 starting bounties/2 starting stacks, means their Bounty Factor is 1.5. If that same player has 30,000 chips and $300 in starting bounties (3/3) their Bounty Factor is 1 again. If he takes a massive hit and goes down to 10,000 chips (3/1) his Bounty Factor is 3. If he goes on an upswing and gets to 60,000 chips without busting anyone (3/6) his Bounty Factor is 0.5.

The ratio is what is important not the size of the bounty. Calling off three stacks to win three bounties is the same as calling off one stack to win one bounty. If a player has doubled up but not won a bounty their bounty factor has halved. If a player has tripled up and won three bounties his bounty factor is 1. If a player has got short, ⅕ of a starting stack, and still has a starting bounty his factor is five.

Bounty Discount

The higher your opponent's Bounty Factor the wider you can call them all-in. Even without doing any further calculations you have probably seen plenty of intuitive examples where you have only had to risk a few chips to pick up a relatively juicy bounty, as well as spots where it would cost you everything to pick up a small one. So how do we use Bounty Factor in the moment at the tables?

The bigger the Bounty Factor, the bigger discount we get on the required equity to call an all-in. We have created a table of Bounty Discounts you can use in-game where you can roughly compare your Bounty Factor to get the required discount. This figure is an approximation and depends on a lot of variables such as the stage of the tournament, blind level and how many players have been eliminated. However, as approximations go it is very reliable, in extensive testing it was never more than 1% wrong. For example, a Bounty Factor of 1 gives a discount of between 5.1% and 5.7%, so we averaged this to 5.4%. This, we believe, is a small enough margin of error to comfortably ignore it.

This is the table of Bounty Discounts, which we suggest you screencap and keep somewhere handy when you are playing:

Bounty Factor	Bounty Discount	Bounty Factor	Bounty Discount	Bounty Factor	Bounty Discount
0.3	1%	1.5	7.4%	4	15.5%
0.4	1.7%	1.75	8.5%	5	17.5%
0.5	3%	2	9.4%	10	25%
0.75	4.2%	2.25	10.2%	20	32%
1	5.4%	2.5	11.1%	50	40%
1.25	6.2%	3	12.7%	100	50%

The Bounty Discount is the amount you can subtract from the equity you need to call profitably. This is why it is so important to develop a baseline understanding of the equities you need to call against standard ranges.

We are going to look at a number of hand examples using this shorthand way of calculating the equity we need, but let's do a simple example you will often find yourself facing to start with.

It is folded to the Button who shoves for 12 big blinds, the Small Blind folds and we are the Big Blind. We have to call 11 big blinds to win a pot of 25.5 big blinds (assuming antes add up to one big blind).

Again in a standard MTT spot with no ICM it would be:

$$11/25.5 * 100 = 43.1\%$$

As we mentioned in the equities chapter, assuming the Button is pushing a wide range then we might be able to call based on these equities. As you can see we can call with any Ax, 22+, K8s+, KTo+ and QTs.

	A	K	Q	J	T	9	8	7	6	5	4	3	2
A	86%	66%	63%	61%	59%	55%	53%	51%	49%	49%	48%	48%	47%
K	65%	77%	52%	51%	49%	46%	43%	42%	41%	41%	40%	39%	39%
Q	61%	50%	72%	46%	44%	41%	39%	38%	38%	37%	37%	36%	36%
J	59%	48%	43%	68%	43%	40%	39%	38%	37%	36%	36%	35%	34%
T	57%	46%	41%	39%	65%	41%	39%	38%	37%	36%	35%	35%	34%
9	53%	42%	38%	37%	37%	61%	40%	39%	38%	36%	35%	34%	33%
8	50%	40%	36%	35%	36%	36%	58%	40%	39%	37%	35%	34%	33%
7	48%	39%	35%	34%	35%	36%	36%	56%	39%	38%	36%	35%	33%
6	46%	38%	34%	33%	34%	34%	35%	36%	54%	39%	37%	35%	34%
5	46%	37%	34%	33%	32%	33%	33%	34%	35%	52%	38%	36%	35%
4	45%	37%	33%	32%	32%	31%	32%	33%	34%	34%	52%	36%	34%
3	45%	36%	33%	31%	31%	30%	30%	31%	32%	33%	32%	48%	33%
2	44%	35%	32%	31%	30%	30%	30%	29%	30%	31%	30%	29%	45%

But let's now assume this is a PKO and that our opponent has a Bounty Factor of 1. Let's just say their 12 big blinds are the starting stack and they have a single bounty. That would give us a Bounty Discount of 5.4%, meaning instead of calling with 43.1% we can in fact call with 36.7% equity.

Looking at that same table, now our calling range becomes Ax, 22+, K4o+, K2s+, Q9o+, Q4s+, J9o+, J6s+, T9o+, T6s+, 96s+, 85s+. 75s+, 64s+, 54s+.

We have gone from only calling with the upper quadrant of our range to being able to profitably call with 54s, and that is just to win a starting bounty.

One more extreme example before we look at this in more depth. Let's say that this 12 big blind shove is again the starting stack, but our opponent has four starting bounties (4/1), giving them a Bounty Factor of 4. Once again, consulting the Bounty Discount table that gives us a discount of 15.5%. We only required 43.1% equity in a standard MTT example so if we subtract that 15.5% then our new required equity to call is just 27.6%.

You don't need to look back at the table, that means against this range we can call with 100% of hands. Even 7-2 offsuit has 30% equity against this range making it just as much a snap call as Pocket Aces.

Remember this is using an example where a player has shoved a relatively wide range with just 12 big blinds, this doesn't mean that every hand will be a snap call when the bounty looks juicy. It does, however, show just how widely we can call in a lot of situations that would be snap folds in a regular MTT. This should also give you some insight into how fold equity is affected when you are the player at risk of elimination. If you have a high Bounty Factor, don't expect many bluffs to get through.

Before we move onto a variety of example hands, let's just take one more look at that table of Bounty Discounts again.

Bounty Factor	Bounty Discount	Bounty Factor	Bounty Discount	Bounty Factor	Bounty Discount
0.3	1%	1.5	7.4%	4	15.5%
0.4	1.7%	1.75	8.5%	5	17.5%
0.5	3%	2	9.4%	10	25%
0.75	4.2%	2.25	10.2%	20	32%
1	5.4%	2.5	11.1%	50	40%
1.12	6.2%	3	12.7%	100	50%

There are a few things to note. First of all that once you get to a Bounty Factor of 0.5 it starts to have an impact on your ranges. A Bounty Factor of 1 is what everyone has at the start of a PKO and that already means we can call an all-in with 5.4% less equity than usual. Once you get to a Bounty Factor of 2 (which could be as simple as a player losing half their stack or winning one bounty) we can start to call with hands that would look ludicrous in a regular tournament. A Bounty Factor of 10 makes almost anything a call in almost any situation. The Bounty Factor examples of 50 and 100 at the end of the table look silly but highlight some extreme examples including when a player gets crippled to a micro stack and also are relevant for when ICM becomes a factor.

We are aware that using a chart like this in-game feels like a paint-by-numbers way of playing poker. It was the simplest way we could allow you to calculate the Bounty Discount in the moment and after a small amount of time should be second nature to you.

I came up with the Bounty Discount concept when I started doing calculations on the equity you need to get your money in the middle of the table on the first hand of a PKO, when both players can win the bounty from each other. I kept doing different calculations and kept noticing that the equity was always 46.2%

to 46.7% on the first hand of the PKO, which I thought was a function of it being early. Then I started reviewing hands later in the tournaments, with different stack sizes and bounties. Regardless of the stage of the tournament I noticed when the starting stack and starting bounties were 1:1, it was always in the region of 46% equity needed to call a player you covered. Whether it was two starting stack and two starting bounties, or five starting stacks and five starting bounties, it was always the same, which led me to ask why that was. I realised it was the ratio of starting stack to starting bounty that was important. I did more experiments with different ratios like 2:1 or 5:2 and worked at that you could always nail them down to a typical equity discount.

I noticed this pattern because I ran a lot of sims, then when I spotted the pattern and ran a bunch of sims to try and disprove it. This is how I recommend people try to learn PKOs, I don't think players should just blindly follow these discount tables. Once you have studied these tables, you should not need to use them at the tables because you should have reviewed your hands after a session often enough that they are second nature.

I went the entire year while writing this book thinking we were particularly clever for crafting the Bounty Discount formula, assuming it to be unique. At the proofreading stage of the book we discovered that legendary poker coach Benjamin 'bencb' Rolle uses a near identical formula in his *Raise Your Edge 'Bounty Beast'* course. It was developed by theoretical physicist "w3cray" and rather than 'Bounty Factor/Bounty Discount' they call it 'Bounty Power/Equity Drop'. There are some small variations but it practically is the same thing. It was frustrating to discover something I developed independently had already been devised by somebody else, but it was gratifying to see that the maths held up and from a theoretical physicist no less. We have no doubt that the Raise Your Edge course would be a great addition to your PKO education.

75/25 and 70/30 Bounty Payouts

At the time of writing most major operators have a 50/50 ratio of immediate payouts and future payouts for the starting bounty, meaning that if you eliminate a player with a $100 bounty, you win $50 right away and $50 goes on your head as your own bounty. There are, however, operators who offer a 70/30 or 75/25 ratio, whereby if you bust a player with a $100 bounty you win $70 or $75 right away, with just $30 or $25 going on your own bounty.

We have looked at the numbers and as an approximation this tends to only add about 0.2% onto the Bounty Discount in-game. For the small Bounty Discounts this doesn't make much of a difference, for example if the Bounty Factor was 1 your Bounty Discount goes from 5.4% to 6.48%, which is unlikely to change your range dramatically. However, as the Bounty Factor gets bigger this 0.2% has a more profound impact. A Bounty Factor of 3, for example, will see the Bounty Discount go from 12.7% to 15.4%. A Bounty Factor of 10 sees it go from 25% to 30%, although we are in the territory of calling our entire range by then anyway.

Practically speaking we think you can still follow the Bounty Discount recommendations we have given for a 50/50 in a 70/30 or 75/25, and just lean a little bit towards the wider end of the calling range. PKOs are such a new format you can expect them to change a lot in the first few years after this book is published, but we still believe using the foundations for the 50/50 bounty structures will be right often enough that you can follow them until your own further study takes over your decision making.

Key takeaways

- The ratio of starting stacks to starting bounties determines how much wider you can call

- Learn your equity against standard ranges first before you start applying the Bounty Discount
- The aim is to internalise the rough discounts in these tables rather than using them forever while you play

Chapter 6. Calling as the coverer

The calculation we gave you in the last chapter is technically all you need to get started but because it is such a massive adjustment from normal MTT strategy it's important to go through some examples as well as explore its limitations. Just as in our first book the bubble of a satellite was such a paradigm shift that we devoted the most time to it, the same is true of calling all-ins in PKOs. It's not enough to know that you should be calling wider in PKOs, you have to get a baseline understanding of how wide, why you can call so wide and also when to tighten up.

For the most part your calling ranges when you are the player who is covered do not change much in PKOs, because you cannot win a bounty, however, they will change slightly because the shoving ranges will be different, which we will cover later.

So let's look at some of the most common calling spots you will face as the coverer.

First hand of a PKO

Let's start with the first of many tricky decisions you will face in a PKO, getting all your money in the middle on the very first hand of the tournament. This is a unique spot in PKOs because everybody has the same stack, same bounty and thus the same Bounty Factor of 1. There is also a notable advantage to the first player to eliminate another player because they become the most likely player to bust the next player, and so on. Nobody wants to risk elimination on the first hand of any tournament but it happens a lot in PKOs, so this is a good first scenario to master.

The numbers in this hand and this chapter differ from the similar examples we saw in Chapter 5, because this time we are factoring in the pot size, which we did not for simplicity last time.

Let's assume it's a $215 PKO with a $100 bounty and 10,000 starting chips, which is 100 big blinds. You are the Big Blind, for argument's sake the Button has open shoved, the Small Blind has folded and you are considering calling. It costs you 99 blinds to win a pot of 200.5 big blinds.

$$99/200.5*100 = 49.4\%$$

Normally in an MTT we expect a tight range for our opponent on the first hand if they are all-in, so let's assume they have 66+ and AT+. This is what our hands would look like against that range:

	A	K	Q	J	T	9	8	7	6	5	4	3	2
A	85%	56%	50%	43%	37%	33%	33%	32%	31%	32%	32%	32%	31%
K	54%	71%	39%	38%	37%	36%	34%	34%	33%	33%	33%	33%	32%
Q	47%	36%	66%	38%	36%	36%	34%	32%	32%	32%	32%	31%	31%
J	40%	34%	34%	60%	36%	36%	34%	32%	31%	31%	31%	30%	30%
T	33%	33%	33%	33%	54%	36%	34%	33%	31%	30%	29%	29%	29%
9	30%	32%	32%	32%	32%	49%	35%	34%	32%	31%	30%	30%	29%
8	29%	31%	30%	30%	30%	32%	46%	34%	32%	31%	30%	29%	29%
7	28%	31%	29%	29%	29%	30%	30%	42%	33%	32%	30%	29%	27%
6	27%	30%	28%	27%	27%	28%	29%	29%	39%	32%	32%	29%	28%
5	29%	29%	28%	27%	26%	27%	28%	28%	28%	38%	32%	30%	29%
4	28%	29%	28%	27%	26%	26%	26%	26%	27%	28%	37%	30%	29%
3	28%	29%	27%	26%	25%	26%	25%	25%	26%	27%	27%	37%	28%
2	27%	28%	27%	26%	25%	35%	25%	24%	24%	25%	25%	25%	36%

In a normal MTT spot we are not particularly happy until we have TT+ and AK. AQs is profitable but only barely.

Now let's apply the Bounty Factor, which is 1 in this spot because we are up against one bounty/one starting stack. Let's consult that all-important Bounty Discount table:

Bounty Factor	Bounty Discount	Bounty Factor	Bounty Discount	Bounty Factor	Bounty Discount
0.3	1%	1.5	7.4%	4	15.5%
0.4	1.7%	1.75	8.5%	5	17.5%
0.5	3%	2	9.4%	10	25%
0.75	4.2%	2.25	10.2%	20	32%
1	5.4%	2.5	11.1%	50	40%
1.25	6.2%	3	12.7%	100	50%

We can remove a Bounty Discount of 5.4% from the 49.4% equity we need to call, meaning we can now call the shove with 44% equity instead. Now AQ, 99 and 88 become calls in this range too. So on the first hand, the calling ranges do not change much if the player population's ranges are similar to what we would expect in a normal MTT.

However, in a lot of PKOs you tend to see some crazy things on the first hand. In some of the lower stakes PKOs you see things that are akin to the old rebuy tournaments back in the day where everyone is going nuts with suited connectors and broadway hands. If, and this is a big if, you have a general read about the player population getting it in much wider, you can adjust your ranges. For example, if you think your opponent would stack off with a wider range of A2s+, A4o+, KQo, KTs+ and 33+ then this is how your hands performs against that range:

	A	K	Q	J	T	9	8	7	6	5	4	3	2
A	86%	64%	60%	57%	53%	49%	46%	44%	42%	41%	40%	39%	39%
K	62%	73%	44%	42%	41%	39%	38%	37%	37%	36%	36%	35%	35%
Q	58%	41%	69%	42%	41%	39%	38%	36%	36%	36%	35%	34%	34%
J	54%	39%	39%	66%	42%	40%	39%	37%	36%	35%	34%	34%	34%
T	51%	38%	38%	39%	63%	41%	39%	38%	36%	35%	34%	34%	33%
9	47%	36%	36%	37%	38%	60%	40%	38%	37%	35%	33%	33%	33%
8	44%	34%	34%	35%	36%	36%	57%	39%	37%	36%	34%	33%	33%
7	41%	34%	33%	34%	34%	35%	35%	55%	38%	36%	34%	33%	32%
6	38%	33%	33%	32%	33%	33%	34%	34%	52%	37%	35%	34%	32%
5	38%	33%	32%	32%	31%	32%	32%	33%	33%	50%	36%	34%	33%
4	37%	32%	31%	30%	30%	30%	30%	31%	31%	32%	46%	33%	32%
3	36%	31%	31%	30%	30%	30%	29%	29%	30%	31%	30%	44%	32%
2	35%	31%	30%	30%	30%	29%	29%	28%	28%	29%	28%	28%	43%

Again, with that discounted range of 44% equity you can call profitably with A8+, KQs, A7s+ and 33+.

This is why it is so important to understand how hands perform against different ranges and why you should be studying independently with equity calculators. The Bounty Discount is useless if you don't have a baseline equity to discount, as well as a good understanding of how different player populations adjust in PKOs. You will see at every buy-in level there are players who treat a PKO like a regular MTT and players who treat it like roulette. If nothing else, doing the hard work now on equities against different ranges will prepare you well for all poker formats, including standard MTTs and cash games, so there is no excuse not to do it.

Sticking with hypothetical 100 big blind spots for a moment, let's just quickly give the player we cover three starting bounties instead of one, all other details the same. So they have a Bounty Factor of 3 instead of 1 (3 starting bounties/1 starting stack).

That gives us a Bounty Discount of 12.7% meaning we can call with just 36.7% equity.

Now in the examples above, even against the tight ranges we can call with AJ+, ATs+, 33+, KJo+, KTs+ and QJs. Against the wider range we can call with 22+, A4o+, A2s+, KTo+ and a ton of suited connectors. We can even call as low as 56s. This is a stark example where we can reliably say that it is correct to call knowing we are behind because the bounty and chance to win future bounties makes this profitable overall.

A small stack shoves

The first example was simplified as in reality it is unlikely the Button would just open shove against you for 100 big blinds. Now let's look at a more common scenario where you call an open shove, which is when an opponent gets short.

We'll continue with the $215 PKO example with $100 bounties, 10,000 starting stacks and 100 big blinds. This time let's assume our opponent is in the Cutoff has one starting bounty and just 5,000 chips. It is now the 200/400 level so they have 12.5 big blinds. They shove, the Button and Small Blind fold and we are pondering a call.

It would cost us 11.5 big blinds to win a pot of 25.5 (no antes in these examples).

$$11.5/25.5*100 = 45\%.$$

Let's say we expect them to do this with anything with better-than-average equity, so perhaps their range looks like A2+, K8o+, K2s+, Q8s+, Q9o+, JTo+, J9s+ and 22+.

Against that range this is how every hand performs:

	A	K	Q	J	T	9	8	7	6	5	4	3	2
A	86%	66%	63%	61%	59%	55%	53%	51%	49%	49%	48%	48%	47%
K	65%	77%	52%	51%	49%	46%	43%	42%	41%	41%	40%	39%	39%
Q	61%	50%	72%	46%	44%	41%	39%	38%	38%	37%	37%	36%	36%
J	59%	48%	43%	68%	43%	40%	39%	38%	37%	36%	36%	35%	34%
T	57%	46%	41%	39%	65%	41%	39%	38%	37%	36%	35%	35%	34%
9	53%	42%	38%	37%	37%	61%	40%	39%	38%	36%	35%	34%	33%
8	50%	40%	36%	35%	36%	36%	58%	40%	39%	37%	35%	34%	33%
7	48%	39%	35%	34%	35%	36%	36%	56%	39%	38%	36%	35%	33%
6	46%	38%	34%	33%	34%	34%	35%	36%	54%	39%	37%	35%	34%
5	46%	37%	34%	33%	32%	33%	33%	34%	35%	52%	38%	36%	35%
4	45%	37%	33%	32%	32%	31%	32%	33%	34%	34%	52%	36%	34%
3	45%	36%	33%	31%	31%	30%	30%	31%	32%	33%	32%	48%	33%
2	44%	35%	32%	31%	30%	30%	30%	29%	30%	31%	30%	29%	45%

In a standard non–ICM non–bounty scenario we can call with hands as weak as A3o, A2s, 22, KTo, K9s, QJo, QTs.

However, there is the small matter of the bounty. The small stack got whittled down to 5,000 which is half a starting stack so their Bounty Factor is 2 (1/0.5). We won't display this table every time but just a reminder, that gives us a Bounty Discount of 9.4%.

Bounty Factor	Bounty Discount	Bounty Factor	Bounty Discount	Bounty Factor	Bounty Discount
0.3	1%	1.5	7.4%	4	15.5%
0.4	1.7%	1.75	8.5%	5	17.5%
0.5	3%	2	9.4%	10	25%
0.75	4.2%	2.25	10.2%	20	32%
1	5.4%	2.5	11.1%	50	40%
1.25	6.2%	3	12.7%	100	50%

Instead we can call with 36.6% equity (45% - 9.4%). That widens our range to include hands as weak as K4o, Q9o, Q4s, J7s and 54s. The fact that we are risking half a starting stack to win a full starting bounty makes it suddenly profitable to call with anything with reasonable equity.

A reminder that it is the ratio that determines the Bounty Factor and thus Bounty Discount. If the same player shoves with the same range with a 10,000 stack and two starting bounties at the 400/800 level, this calculation is exactly the same.

It is still 11.5 big blinds to win a pot of 25.5.

$$11.5/25.5*100 = 45\%.$$

It is still 2 starting bounties/1 starting stack = Bounty Factor 2, which gives you a Bounty Discount of 9.4%

So your calling range would still be hands with 36.6% equity or better.

Small Blind shoves into Big Blind

Just for fun, and this happens a lot, let's just look at how wide we can call when we know the ranges are exceptionally wide to begin with. All other details are as before, but this time the Small Blind shoves into the Big Blind for 10,000 chips at the 400/800 level. It would cost us 11.5 big blinds to win a 25 big blind pot, assuming no antes.

11.5/25*100 = 46%.

We can expect the Small Blind to shove very wide against us, something like this 22+, A2+, K2s+, K8o+, Q4s+, Q8o+, J6s+, J8o+, T6s+, T8o+, 95s+, 98o+, 84s+ , 87o, 74s+, 76o, 63s+, 53s+ and 43s.

As you can imagine, against such a wide range we can call with just about all coordinated hands or high cards.

	A	K	Q	J	T	9	8	7	6	5	4	3	2
A	84%	66%	64%	62%	61%	58%	57%	55%	53%	53%	52%	51%	51%
K	64%	78%	57%	56%	54%	52%	50%	49%	48%	47%	46%	46%	45%
Q	62%	55%	75%	53%	52%	49%	47%	45%	45%	44%	43%	42%	42%
J	60%	53%	50%	72%	50%	47%	45%	43%	42%	42%	41%	40%	40%
T	59%	52%	49%	47%	69%	46%	44%	43%	41%	40%	39%	39%	38%
9	56%	49%	46%	44%	43%	65%	43%	42%	41%	39%	38%	37%	37%
8	55%	47%	44%	42%	41%	40%	62%	42%	40%	39%	37%	36%	35%
7	52%	46%	42%	40%	39%	39%	38%	58%	40%	39%	37%	36%	35%
6	51%	45%	41%	39%	38%	37%	37%	37%	56%	39%	38%	36%	35%
5	50%	44%	41%	38%	36%	36%	35%	36%	36%	53%	38%	37%	35%
4	49%	43%	40%	38%	36%	34%	33%	34%	34%	35%	51%	36%	35%
3	48%	42%	39%	37%	35%	34%	32%	32%	33%	34%	33%	49%	34%
2	48%	42%	39%	36%	35%	33%	31%	31%	31%	31%	31%	31%	47%

It probably doesn't need exploring any further but let's just say the Small Blind has one starting bounty, giving them a Bounty Factor of 1 (1 starting bounty/1 starting stack). As you will no doubt recall that gives us a Bounty Discount of 5.4% taking the required equity to call down from 46% to 40.6%. That means we can call as wide as K2o, Q2s, J4s, Q5o and 87s.

Give that same player two starting bounties and it gives them a Bounty Factor of 2 (2 starting bounties/1 starting stack) and the discount is 9.4%, meaning we our calling equity goes from 46% to 36.6%. Again, at this stage there is very little we don't call with.

We could go on but basically when the cost of calling is low in chip terms, pretty much anything is a justifiable call.

20x starting stack x3 bounties

At this stage it might be looking like if you add a bounty to the mix, everything becomes a snap call. However, once again, it really is about the ratio of starting bounty to starting stack. Back to that same $215 PKO with 10,000 starting chips and a $100 starting bounty. Let's say this time we have run our stack up over 100,000 and face another player who has done the same, who has 100,000 themselves and $300 in bounties. The blinds are 5,000/10,000 and we are facing a shove from the Button as the Big Blind after the Small Blind folds.

So it costs us nine big blinds to win a pot of 20.5 big blinds, assuming no antes.

$$9/20.5*100 = 44\%$$

We need 44% equity to call and we put them on a range of A2s+, A4o+, KQo, KTs+ and 33+, so this is how our hands perform against that range:

	A	K	Q	J	T	9	8	7	6	5	4	3	2
A	86%	64%	60%	57%	53%	49%	46%	44%	42%	41%	40%	39%	39%
K	62%	73%	44%	42%	41%	39%	38%	37%	37%	36%	36%	35%	35%
Q	58%	41%	69%	42%	41%	39%	38%	36%	36%	36%	35%	34%	34%
J	54%	39%	39%	66%	42%	40%	39%	37%	36%	35%	34%	34%	34%
T	51%	38%	38%	39%	63%	41%	39%	38%	36%	35%	34%	34%	33%
9	47%	36%	36%	37%	38%	60%	40%	38%	37%	35%	33%	33%	33%
8	44%	34%	34%	35%	36%	36%	57%	39%	37%	36%	34%	33%	33%
7	41%	34%	33%	34%	34%	35%	35%	55%	38%	36%	34%	33%	32%
6	38%	33%	33%	32%	33%	33%	34%	34%	52%	37%	35%	34%	32%
5	38%	33%	32%	32%	31%	32%	32%	33%	33%	50%	36%	34%	33%
4	37%	32%	31%	30%	30%	30%	30%	31%	31%	32%	46%	33%	32%
3	36%	31%	31%	30%	30%	30%	29%	29%	30%	31%	30%	44%	32%
2	35%	31%	30%	30%	30%	29%	29%	28%	28%	29%	28%	28%	43%

However, we are in a PKO and our opponent has three starting bounties and ten starting stacks (3/10) and thus a Bounty Factor of 0.3. If we consult that (now becoming very familiar) conversion table, we will see that....

Bounty Factor	Bounty Discount	Bounty Factor	Bounty Discount	Bounty Factor	Bounty Discount
0.3	1%	1.5	7.4%	4	15.5%
0.4	1.7%	1.75	8.5%	5	17.5%
0.5	3%	2	9.4%	10	25%
0.75	4.2%	2.25	10.2%	20	32%
1	5.4%	2.5	11.1%	50	40%
1.25	6.2%	3	12.7%	100	50%

It does widen our range, but not by a degree many would expect. We get a Bounty Discount of 1%, meaning we can call with 43% equity instead of 44%. Against the assumed range we have assigned, the only extra hand we can call with because of the Bounty Discount is 22. Just as how wide we can call in some spots may surprise some of the tighter players reading this, just how little our ranges change in spots like this will surprise the looser players among you. A lot of players will see three starting bounties for *just* ten big blinds and think this was the easiest call in poker, when in reality our range does not change.

The reason why this is not a super wide call will make sense to those of you familiar with ICM and we will explore it more in our chapter on the payout and final table stages. It may just be ten big blinds but the later the tournament goes the more each chip is worth to you. Punting off ten big blinds for a bounty is probably never going to be a mistake in the first level of a tournament when stacks are deep, doing the same thing later on when the average stacks are much shallower, and especially with the payouts on the horizon, is a much more costly mistake.

3-bet pot/4-bet pot

All the examples so far have been when we face an open shove, let's look at the other frequent preflop occurrence where we face an all-in call, which is when we open raise and get shoved over, or when we reraise ourselves and get 4-bet all-in by our opponent.

Once again, a $215 PKO with 10,000 starting stacks and it is the 200/400 level. We open to 2.5 big blinds from the Button and the Small Blind shoves for 10,000, the Big Blind folds.

In this spot it would cost us 22.5 big blinds to win a potential pot of 51.

*22.5/51*100=44%.*

We need 44% equity to call and we are putting our opponent on a tight range of 66+ and ATo. This is how the hands perform against that range:

amazon Gift Receipt

Send a Thank You Note

You can learn more about your gift or start a return here too.

Scan using the Amazon app or visit
https://a.co/d/04dY6ae

PKO Poker Strategy: How to adapt to Bounty and Progressive Knockout online poker tournaments (The Poker Solved Series)

Order ID: 111-8593866-5673005 Ordered on January 5, 2024

SQfmSNtmpk

amazon.com

Purchase Order #: Zip Books FY23-24
Order of January 5, 2024

Qty. Item

PKO Poker Strategy: How to adapt to Bounty and Progressive Knockout online poker tournaments (The Poker Solved Series)
O'Kearney, Dara --- Paperback
1527262774
1527262774 9781527262775

Return or replace your item
Visit Amazon.com/returns

SQfmSNtmpk/-2 of 2-//SMF5-TWI/next-1dc/0/0106-23:00/0106-08:13

B1-
M8

amazon.com

A gift for you

Enclosed is your Zip Book. When finished, please return the item and note to the desk of any Sacramento Public Library. From Sacramento Public Library Zip Book

	A	K	Q	J	T	9	8	7	6	5	4	3	2
A	85%	56%	50%	43%	37%	33%	33%	32%	31%	32%	32%	32%	31%
K	54%	71%	39%	38%	37%	36%	34%	34%	33%	33%	33%	33%	32%
Q	47%	36%	66%	38%	36%	36%	34%	32%	32%	32%	32%	31%	31%
J	40%	34%	34%	60%	36%	36%	34%	32%	31%	31%	31%	30%	30%
T	33%	33%	33%	33%	54%	36%	34%	33%	31%	30%	29%	29%	29%
9	30%	32%	32%	32%	32%	49%	35%	34%	32%	31%	30%	30%	29%
8	29%	31%	30%	30%	30%	32%	46%	34%	32%	31%	30%	29%	29%
7	28%	31%	29%	29%	29%	30%	30%	42%	33%	32%	30%	29%	27%
6	27%	30%	28%	27%	27%	28%	29%	29%	39%	32%	32%	29%	28%
5	29%	29%	28%	27%	26%	27%	28%	28%	28%	38%	32%	30%	29%
4	28%	29%	28%	27%	26%	26%	26%	26%	27%	28%	37%	30%	29%
3	28%	29%	27%	26%	25%	26%	25%	25%	26%	27%	27%	37%	28%
2	27%	28%	27%	26%	25%	35%	25%	24%	24%	25%	25%	25%	36%

Now let's assume the same player has three starting bounties of $300 (3/1) giving them a Bounty Factor of 3. That gives us a Bounty Discount of 12.7%, meaning we can actually call them with 31.3% equity.

It would seem insane to call off so wide preflop against a 3-bet shove which by definition usually means a very strong range, but even knowing how narrow our opponent could be we can still justifiably call with hands like K9o and 56s. This is before you even begin to factor in that the 3-betting ranges tend to be wider in PKOs as a rule. They may also be capped, meaning some regulars would be more likely to flat call with AA or KK to induce more action.

If the action is the same but instead it is the 2,000/4,000 level and our opponent shoves for 100,000 (ten starting stacks) and three starting bounties, that gives them a bounty factor of 0.3 and a Bounty Discount of 1%. Again that does widen our equity from

44% to 43%, which barely changes our ranges at all. We are risking the same effective stacks, but not the same starting stacks.

Against two bounties

One of the most exciting prospects in the early to middle stages of a PKO is when multiple players have gone all-in and you cover all of them, thus you can win several bounties.

Before we go further, let's just look at standard equities against two standard (20%) ranges. It could certainly be the case that at least one of the players (the one that covers the shortest stack) is much wider, but let's err on the side of caution.

	A	K	Q	J	T	9	8	7	6	5	4	3	2
A	67%	39%	36%	34%	32%	29%	27%	25%	24%	24%	22%	22%	21%
K	36%	60%	37%	34%	33%	31%	29%	28%	27%	26%	25%	25%	24%
Q	33%	33%	54%	35%	34%	31%	29%	27%	26%	26%	25%	24%	24%
J	31%	31%	31%	49%	33%	30%	28%	27%	25%	24%	23%	23%	23%
T	29%	30%	30%	30%	45%	30%	29%	27%	25%	23%	22%	22%	22%
9	26%	27%	27%	27%	28%	40%	28%	27%	25%	23%	21%	21%	20%
8	25%	25%	25%	26%	26%	26%	37%	27%	25%	23%	21%	20%	20%
7	23%	24%	23%	24%	24%	25%	25%	34%	26%	24%	22%	20%	19%
6	21%	24%	23%	22%	23%	23%	24%	24%	32%	25%	23%	21%	20%
5	21%	23%	22%	22%	20%	21%	22%	22%	23%	29%	23%	21%	20%
4	20%	23%	21%	21%	20%	19%	20%	20%	21%	21%	26%	20%	19%
3	18%	21%	20%	20%	19%	19%	18%	18%	19%	20%	19%	25%	18%
2	18%	20%	20%	20%	19%	18%	18%	17%	17%	18%	17%	16%	24%

As you can see, most hands go down in value by virtue of the fact that we are competing with more hole cards, but that is offset by the fact that the chips and bounties on offer are laying us a very good price to call.

So let's start out assuming we are covering a 10 big blind shove with 10,000 chips which is then isolated by a 20 big blind stack with 20,000 chips, both have the starting bounty. The Small Blind folds and we are the Big Blind.

$$19/50.5*100 = 38\%.$$

Even though the pot is laying us a good price, we need a very strong hand to call in a normal MTT situation because we are up against two likely strong hands. So in this spot 99+ and AKs are calls.

When you add them up we are also fighting for two starting bounties and three starting stacks (2/3) giving us a Bounty Factor of 0.66, which roughly removes 3% from the 38% we need to call with. That doesn't really change much, we can call with AQs now but that's about it.

Let's replay the same scenario but give the shorter player three starting bounties and the 20 big blind stack three starting bounties. The chips are the same, three starting stacks, so it's 6/3 giving us a Bounty Factor of 2. That means we can remove 9.4% from the required 38%, meaning we can call with just 28.6% equity. Against two strongish hands that still doesn't mean we can call with junk like low connectors or weak Kings, but we can call an all-in and a call profitably with a hand like K8s or 55.

The Eureka moment here should be that whether it is one opponent, two or five, calculating Bounty Factor and Bounty Discount is the same across the board. It's about the ratio between starting stacks and starting bounties. As long as you understand how equities change in general in multiway pots so that you don't stack off as light as you would against one player, the adjustment remains the same.

Post flop spots

All of the examples have been preflop so far because they are easier to quantify and in the medium to late stages of PKOs, like any MTT, it is mostly a preflop game. However, nothing is different in principle postflop. If you cover your opponent and are facing an all-in call, as long as you have a foundational understanding of the equity you need to make a profitable ChipEV call, the Bounty Factor and Bounty Discounts are the same. If you need 44% equity to call preflop but your opponent's Bounty Factor is 2 meaning your discounted equity is 34.6%, that will also be true if you need 44% equity to call them on the flop.

Let's look at a couple of examples, this time it's easier to look at specific hands rather than our range. Let's assume there are 20 big blinds effective behind and 5.5 big blinds in the middle of the table. The flop is A-7-6 rainbow we continuation bet for 3 big blinds with KK, and our opponent then reraises all-in for 20 big blinds.

We don't think they are bluffing and put them on a range of AK, AQ, AJ, AT, A7, A6, 67 and 89 (a semi bluff). We think they would slowplay AA so have discounted that.

Calculating the equity we need to call is the same as preflop.

$$17/45.5*100 = 37\%$$

Our hands only have 20% equity against that range which is little surprise, you already know how much a hand like KK shrinks in value when an Ace flops and there is action. However, let's assume our opponent has 10,000 chips (a starting stack as per all our examples) and five starting bounties (5/1). Their Bounty Factor of 5 gives them a Bounty Discount of 17.5%, meaning we can actually call with 19.5% equity. The ratio of starting stacks to starting bounties means that we can knowingly get our money in almost certainly behind because we outdraw them often enough to make this a profitable call.

Let's flip things around and look at the same spot, but this time we have 89o facing that 20 big blind shove, meaning we have an open ended straight draw. In a normal MTT spot with only 33% equity, this would be a bad call.

However, if our opponent has a 10,000 starting stack and two starting bounties (2/1) giving them a Bounty Factor of 2 with a Bounty Discount of 9.4%. We now only need 27.6% equity to call and our straight draw with 33% equity is a very easy call.

We could go on but you get the idea, if the Bounty Discount is big enough there are post flop spots where gutshots, underpairs and high card hands become snap calls. Again, the key here is understanding what your ranges should be in normal MTT spots initially, understanding the discount is pointless if you don't get this bit right.

We are going to look at wet vs dry flops in a later chapter, but until then just understand that the same discounts apply to pre and post flop.

Passing profitable spots

At this stage it might seem like we are advocating for calling very wide whenever a bounty presents itself, which is certainly not the case. In regular tournaments there are plenty of spots which might be profitable to call but for a number of reasons the better advice would be to tread lightly. A classic example might be to pass up a likely coin flip with Ace King when you have an edge over your table. The exact same principles apply in PKOs, although the bounty means you can call wider, there are still good reasons to pass profitable spots because of future equity, that is you will have better opportunities to make money.

If the presence of a bounty means you can call with a hand with 36% equity rather than 44% equity, that doesn't mean you should snap call with anything with 36% equity or better. It is still preferable to have a notable edge, so maybe 38% or better in this example. When you pass profitable spots vs when you take them depends on four factors – your stack size, the structure, your perceived edge and the table situation.

Stack size

If you are short stacked you probably should not be passing any profitable spot, whether you cover or are covered. If, however, you can win a bounty despite being short, this might be the single best shot you have to realise your equity and get back in the game.

If you are deep you should be more conservative with your stack. It may be 'correct' to call wider in a particular spot but risking 100 big blinds to win 0.1 big blinds long term, when the downside is elimination, is going to be very stressful.

If you have more than 15 big blinds you can pass on very close spots and wait for better ones to present themselves.

If you have between 8-14 big blinds you are not really in a position to pass any close spots. Wait any longer and you will get dwindled down to nothing.

If you have less than seven big blinds it often makes sense to take some minus EV spots, especially if there is a bounty on the line. Because so much equity in PKOs is tied up in winning future bounties, you need to put yourself in a position to cover people.

Structure

PKOs are quite fast in nature, but if the structure is slower and deeper than average, you can pass up more marginal spots. You will have more time and more room to outplay your opponents.

If it is a hyper turbo structure you cannot pass any close spots, because an average stack goes to a short stack in just a few orbits of inaction in fast formats.

Perceived edge

The bigger edge you think you have over the field the more conservative you should be. The biggest winners in tournament poker pass the most marginal spots because they don't want to increase variance for little or no upside in terms of EV.

This is perhaps even more important in PKOs while they remain an 'unsolved' format where few people know or study the correct adjustments.

Table situation

The last three factors you are probably aware of and apply to any MTT format, however the makeup of the table in respect to stack and bounty size is a unique consideration in PKOs. Who covers you, whom you cover and what you can win from each other should significantly inform when to pass marginal spots in PKOs.

It's not just about what you can win right now, it is about what will happen to our ability to win bounties if we win or lose.

If, for example, we are short stacked and cover nobody, but winning an all-in means we would cover three people at the table, then we should take any profitable spot. Not only will we win the chips when we win but we will gain the opportunity to claim more bounties. If there is a particularly juicy bounty at the table and doubling up means we cover them, it might even be correct to make a minus EV call so we can cover them.

On the flip-side if we cover everybody at the table and losing an all-in means we would not, it is much better to pass on a marginal spot because we will no doubt find ourselves in better spots. This is especially true if we are facing the prospect of calling the 2nd biggest stack at the table but they only have their starting bounty.

Of course your table can be broken at any moment, so it is important not to be too rigid with these considerations. Broadly speaking, however, it is important to remember how big a factor future equity winning is in PKOs. When you cover everyone at your table you are playing for a bigger prize pool than they are, so while you take more risks to realise your equity immediately in PKOs, protecting your ability to win bounties is just important too.

Key takeaways

- Bounty Discount is useless if you first do not understand what your calling range would be in a regular MTT situation
- When a player's chip stack is low, you can usually call wide for the bounty without much deliberation
- When a player has a lot of starting stacks but not many bounties, the calling ranges are much closer to a regular MTT
- The same Bounty Discount calculations apply for calling multiple opponents who you cover all-in (but remember how equities change multiway)
- Bounty Discount applies to post flop in exactly the same way as preflop
- It can be wise to pass on close, but profitable, bounty spots if the table dynamics make sense to
-

Chapter 7. When ICM IS A FACTOR

By now you will appreciate just how complex any decision in a PKO tournament can be compared to a regular tournament. When ICM and payouts are involved, those layers of complexity increase exponentially. We wrestled with just how to tackle this complexity and we eventually arrived at the brave, or possibly foolish, step of just having one hand example to cover most bubble and final table decisions.

If you have read our previous book on satellites you will recall we covered the endgame quite extensively, with common situations as well as how to adjust in unique spots. The big difference between PKOs and satellites is that you can make perfect assumptions in satellites, because the prizes are of equal value. When you run a sim through an ICM calculator it can give you a definitive answer. You cannot even make perfect assumptions in regular tournaments because the payout structures vary. In a PKO it gets even more complicated because not only do the payout structures vary but you do not know how much of the bounty prize pool is remaining. A simulation for a 100 runner $10,000 guaranteed PKO on Monday will not give the correct answer to an identical spot in a 100 runner $10,000 guaranteed PKO on Tuesday.

This is because of the progressive nature of the bounties. In a traditional bounty tournament with a static bounty the bounty prize pool is just the starting bounties multiplied by the remaining players. In a PKO, however, it can vary greatly because the players who are eliminated have also eliminated other players. Who eliminates whom in a PKO changes the prize pool.

You can be certain of the remaining bounty prize pool when nobody has been eliminated, it is still 100%. You can also be certain of it when the first player has been eliminated, it will be missing half a starting bounty. However, from that point onwards sims become unreliable because the makeup of who busts who can vary. Usually when the second player is eliminated the bounty prize pool is reduced by one starting bounty (to be specific, two half starting bounties), but occasionally the player who won the first bounty loses two big pots in a row and becomes the 2nd player to be eliminated. In that instance it is 1.5 starting bounties, not one, that have been removed from the bounty prize pool. There are extreme examples like if one player knocked everybody out of the tournament (which is not that ridiculous and applicable to PKO SNGs) would mean exactly 75% of the bounty prize pool is gone by the heads-up stage. Other than that, every player removed from the bounty prize pool makes it more complex and thus trying to do accurate sims that give a 'correct' answer to future spots becomes futile.

We did a lot of sims to get an approximation of how much of the bounty prize pool is likely to remain at different stages of the tournament. When you lose half the field, it is guaranteed that 25% of the starting bounties are gone but it averages to around 27%. When you lose ¾ of the field it averages to about 52% of the bounty prize pool gone. When you get down to 12.5% of the field then around 73.5% of the bounty prize pool has been realised, and so on.

This is just an approximation and you will see some extreme outliers. It would be impossible to produce set-in-stone simulations as we did in *Poker Satellite Strategy* and if we tried to replicate all the possible scenarios at the payout stages, we think there would be the potential to bamboozle you with seemingly contradictory information.

Instead we are going to present to you one single hand example, which we will present in four different formats - ChipEV, non ICM PKO, final table non PKO and final table PKO. Rather than trying to give you the template for crushing final tables instead we want to show you how the presence of bounties *change* a typical final table spot. This entire book has been written on the premise that you continue to study regular MTT spots independently, so use this as a guiding principle on how to adjust your normal ranges for a PKO.

One final point to highlight why it's important to look at the way PKOs change a range, rather than the range itself in each particular spot, became apparent to us while we were writing this book. The ICM calculators like ICMIZER and Holdem Resources Calculator are also just coming to terms with PKO tournaments. We noticed that the ranges Holdem Resources Calculator produced changed slightly when we retested them months later. This obviously doesn't mean the math has changed, simply that the solvers are getting more accurate, and will continue to get more accurate.

ICM and PKOs

Before the hand, a quick primer on the Independent Chip Model (ICM). We said at the start of this book that we expect you to have a baseline understanding of ICM and how play differs at the end stage of tournaments when real money payouts are a factor. That hasn't changed, if you really are not familiar with ICM you should brush up on that online before continuing further in this section. However, we will briefly talk about ICM and the unique relationship it has with bounties.

ICM is a model used to calculate your overall equity in a poker tournament and what your chips are currently worth based on the payout structure. It explains how the value of your chip stack changes throughout a tournament. In a cash game if you sit down with $1,000 each chip is worth the actual cash denomination it represents, so a $25 chip is worth $25. Strategically this is what we refer to as a ChipEV situation.

If you sit down in a $1,000 multi table tournament with 100 players in it and a 10,000 starting stack then at the start of that tournament your stack is worth $1,000 (let's assume no rake for this example) and a 1,000 chip is worth $100. However, if you go on to win that 100 person tournament you may only win $30,000 even though there is $100,000 in the prize pool. You have accumulated all the chips but not all the cash. That same 1,000 chip that was worth $100 at the start of the tournament is now actually only worth $30. Where did all the money go? It went to the other players in the form of payouts.

In a standard tournament with normal payouts, the cash value of the chips devalue after every payout. The prize pool shrinks with every bust out but the chips remain in play. The average value of the chips remain the same in the tournament until the bubble. This is why a ChipEV decision (one which would be correct in a cash game or winner takes all tournament) is not necessarily going to be the same as an ICM decision (a decision which is profitable in terms of your tournament equity). A call which would, on average, increase your chips, on the bubble can often be unprofitable in terms of real money payouts. This is because all the times you lose you not only miss out on chips but also a payout, whereas folding keeps you in with a shot at making the money.

This is why in a spot where you normally would need 45% equity to call profitably, you might actually need 65% equity to call profitably on the bubble of a tournament. You need a much better than average hand in ICM spots because the downside is so much greater than ChipEV spots. In *Poker Satellite Strategy* we highlighted a range of examples where the equity you needed to call on the bubble of a satellite was so high that there were literally no hands you could call a shove with. Even Pocket Aces is a preflop fold in some spots in a satellite.

The lesson here is that ICM is a factor that contracts your calling range in the end game stages of a tournament. The bounty in a PKO, as we have seen, has the opposite effect, it expands your calling range. My co-author Barry joked that he got better at PKOs after working on the satellite book because he just did the opposite in PKOs of what he should do in a satellite. PKOs and satellites are two extreme ends of tournament poker and I like to illustrate this by thinking of a dial. A regular tournament might have the dial in the middle, but when the payouts are flat like in a satellite it might move towards one end, but when bounties are involved the dial goes in the opposite direction.

The question is, when payouts are involved in a PKO tournament, where does the dial point? What has the bigger impact on our calling ranges, the ICM or the bounties? That is what we will explore with the following hand example, but before we start please try to think of the ICM dial as a fluid and nuanced thing. In any PKO payout spot, it helps to get back to first principles. Think about what your ranges would be in a normal tournament first, then try to estimate how much the ICM pulls you in one direction and how much the bounties pull you in the other.

One final note before we start which I think might really help hammer home this idea. When I grind online poker and play twelve to sixteen tables at once I use three monitors. I put all the satellites on the left monitor, all the regular MTTs on the middle monitor and all the PKOs on the right monitor. This is to stop me making the mistake of playing one format like the other, but it is also an excellent visual representation of the two pole extremes of ICM. If you play a lot of tables online I advise you to do something similar.

Button vs the Blinds

It's difficult to pick any hand that has broad application to all other hand scenarios, but we think we have picked one which is both common and also highlights enough of what makes PKOs unique to be transferable to a lot of situations. The example is a nine-handed table where the first six players have 20 Big Blinds and it is folded to the Button who has 10 big blinds, the Small Blind has 12 big blinds and the Big Blind who has 20 big blinds. The table looks like this:

500/1,000 (ante 125) level

UTG: 20,000
UTG+1: 20,000
MP1: 20,000
MP2: 20,000
MP3: 20,000
CO: 20,000
BTN: 10,000
SB: 12,000
BB: 20,000

We are going to look at how the Button, Small Blind and Big Blind should play against each other when it is folded to them. In each example we will look at the GTO ranges in a normal ChipEV spot (no bounties), an early PKO spot, a normal final table spot (no bounties) and finally a PKO final table spot. The ChipEV spots are for cash game formats or very early in an MTT. The PKO spots are at the start of a PKO, nobody has been eliminated yet so everyone has a starting bounty. The first final table spots are for regular MTTs (we chose a 90 man SNG on PokerStars which is very much a median payout structure). Finally, for the PKO final table we used a 90 man SNG example again and assumed 73% of the bounties were still in play, with everyone having an average bounty.

The differences alone between these four situations at an otherwise identical table really showcase the impact of both bounties and payouts on our ranges.

All these ranges are assuming everyone is playing Game Theory Optimal and were simulated by an ICM calculator.

To begin with, it is folded around to the Button who has ten big blinds. If they are going to play the hand, they are usually going to shove with it. Let's look at what those shoving ranges should be.

Button 10 BB shoving range	
Format	*Range*
ChipEV	45.3% 22+ Ax K2s+ K5o+ Q4s+ Q9o+ J6s+ J9o+ T6s+ T9o 96s+ 98o 85s+ 75s+ 65s 54s
Early PKO	40.0% 22+ Ax K2s+ K6o+ Q5s+ Q9o+ J7s+ J9o+ T7s 97s 87s
Normal Final Table	41.4% 22+ Ax K2s+ K9o+ Q4s+ Q9o+ J6s+ J9o+ T6s+ T9o+ 96s+ 98o 86s+ 75s+ 65s+ 54s+
PKO Final Table	24.7% 33+ A2s+ A4o+ K8s+ KTo+ Q9s+ QJo JTs

As you can see there is not a great deal of difference between the first three ranges. This is in part because the later you are in position, the more profitable it is to shove because you have less people to get through, so you will get plenty of folds. There is barely any difference between the ChipEV and normal final table ranges. The slight difference between those two and the early PKO example is that the lower suited cards drop out of the range. This is because you are much more likely to get called in the PKO because of the bounty, so your range is weighted more towards hands that are likely to be ahead when called.

The notable difference is what happens at the PKO final table when payouts are involved but also everyone has an average bounty based on the remaining prize pool. The shoving range has dropped from around 40% in the first three examples to 25%. Our range really has shrunk to hands that we can expect to be ahead a lot of the time when called, we don't even shove every Ace. This is a dramatic tightening of the range, because we have three factors compelling us to tighten our range. We have the fact that we are almost certainly going to be called to get our bounty, the fact that right now we cannot win a bounty ourselves and finally the fact that busting out next would mean we miss the next, and future, pay jumps.

One way to understand the shoving ranges in each spot better is to look at what the GTO calling ranges are for that shove. First let's look at the Small Blind's calling range when the Button shoves.

Small Blind calling range	
Format	*Range*
ChipEV	30.1% 22+ Ax K5s+ K9o+ Q9s+ QTo+ J9s T9s
Early PKO	37.0% 22+ Ax K2s+ K7o+ Q6s+ Q9o+ J8s+ JTo+ T8s+ 98s+ 87s+ 76s
Normal Final Table	12.2% 66+ A7s+ A9o+ KJs+ KQo
PKO Final Table	21.2% 33+ A2s+A7o+ K9s+ KTo+ QTs+ QJo+ JTs+ T9s

We have said calling range for simplicity, technically it is the Small Blind's 3-betting range because there is a player left to act. As they only have two big blinds more than the Button, it's essentially a call.

Now in every example we see the ranges diverge massively from each other, the impact of the bounties and payouts are much more profound because when you are calling, you don't have the benefit of fold equity. You have to have the winning hand when you call, and in this example the bounties and payouts dictate just how good your hand has to be.

In the ChipEV example we need the top 30.1% of hands to beat the 45.3% shoving range of the Button. We are weighted towards high cards and pairs that figure to be ahead most of the time anyway.

Early in a PKO we can call with a very wide range of 37% of hands, against the 40% shoving range of the Button. This is the only player we can currently win the bounty from, so they represent our best spot at the table.

At a normal final table the Small Blind can call just 12.2% of the time with the very top end of their range. This is because of the impact of the payouts coupled with the fact that the Big Blind could wake up with a hand and eliminate them. When you are the second shortest stack at the table, it is a disaster to bust out before the shortest stack. This is why the Button can shove wide with 41.4% of their hands, because the Small Blind has to fold a lot.

The interesting spot once again is the PKO Final Table, which has moved the Small Blind's range to 21.2% of hands. They still have to opt for the higher end of their range but they can call with quite speculative hands like T9s. Early in a PKO saw our range go very wide (37%) and a normal final table saw it go very tight (12.2%), but a PKO final table has had a stabilizing effect on our range. The bounty has pulled our range in one direction, the payouts have pulled it in the other, and the impact has almost brought us in line with the regular ChipEV range.

Now let's look at what should happen if the Button shoves and the Small Blind folds. How much wider should the Big Blind call in different spots?

Big Blind calling range	
Format	*Range*
ChipEV	37.8% 22+ Ax K2s+ K6o+ Q6s+ Q9o+ J8s+ J9o T8s 98s
Early PKO	48.1% 22+ Ax K2s+ K3o+ Qs+ Q8o+ J5s+ J9o+ T6s+ T9o+ 96s+ 86s+ 75s+ 65s+ 54s+
Normal Final Table	21.7% 33+ A2s+ A5o+ K9s+ KTo+ QTs+
PKO Final Table	44.4% 22+ Ax K2s+ K8o+ Q5s+ Q9o+ J6s+ J9o+ T6s+ T8o+ 96s+ 98o 85s+ 87o 75s+ 64s+ 54s+

It's no surprise that the Big Blind can call wider than the Small Blind in every scenario. They cover the Button more comfortably, they are getting a better price to call and they get to close the action, so they are not worried about someone acting behind them. Early in a PKO they can call super wide and the same is true at a PKO final table, although it is a 4% less than early in a PKO because ICM is playing a role.

Things get really interesting when we look at the situation where the Button shoves and the Small Blind shoves over the top of them. What is the Big Blind's calling range in each of the situations?

Big Blind calling range vs Button shove and & Small Blind reshove	
Format	*Range*
ChipEV	20.8% 33+ A3s+ A8o+ K9s+ KTo+ Q9s+ QJo J9s T9s
Early PKO	54.4% 22+ Kx Q2s+ Q8o+ J4s+ J8o+ T5s+ T8o+ 95s+ 98o 85s+ 87o 74s+ 64s+ 53s+
Normal Final Table	4.2% 99+ AQs+ AKo
PKO Final Table	51.7% 22+ A2s+ A4o+ K2s+ K9o+ Q2s+ Q8o+ J3s+ J8o+ T4s+ T8o+ 95s+ 97o+ 84s+ 86o+74s+ 76s 76o 63s+ 65o 52s+ 43s

By now you should not be too surprised at the difference between ChipEV and early in a PKO is dramatic. The chance to win two bounties means we can open up our calling range to 49.3% of hands, compared to 20.8%.

The staggering thing to note is the difference between a regular final table and a PKO final table. Although the Big Blind is not at risk, they still need to call the top end of their range (99+, AQs+, AKo) because of the impact of ICM. They need a hand that could beat two other hands without improvement essentially. The same spot in a PKO Final Table sees that range increase from 4.2% to 51.7%. The chance to win two bounties and move up two pay spots more than makes up for the downside of losing the hand. However, ICM does still play a role, as the range is not as wide as the early PKO spot.

The other thing worth noting in both PKO spots is that the ranges are weighted heavily towards suited hands. For example, not every Ace or King is in the PKO Final Table range, but 43s is. This should make intuitive sense, because these are hands that do well multiway. Against one opponent the emphasis is on hands that can win without improvement a lot of the time, but multiway we are expecting to be behind, so hands that can outdraw one pair type hands go up in value.

Small Blind vs Big Blind

While we are here, we may as well take a look at what happens if the Button folds leaving the Small Blind to take on the Big Blind. This is the single most common battle you will have in any poker scenario and typically requires both positions to widen their range, so one would expect in a PKO it would be carnage.

Chip EV Blind vs Blind ranges	
Small Blind shove	69.5% 22+ Qx J2s+ J7o+ T2s+ T7o+ 93s+ 96o+ 84s+ 86o+ 73s+ 76o 63s+ 65o 53s+ 43s
Big Blind call	48.5% 22+ Kx Q2s+ Q6o+ J6s+ J8o+ T7s+ T9o 98s
Early PKO Blind vs Blind ranges	
Small Blind shove	61.5% 22+ Qx J2s+ J7o+ T5s+ T7o+ 95s+ 98o 85s+ 87o 75s+ 64s 54s
Big Blind call	54.9% 22+ Kx Q2s+ Q4o+ J4s+ J7o+ T6s+ T8o+ 96s+ 98o 86s+ 76s+
Normal final table Blind vs Blind ranges	
Small Blind shove	65.3% 22+ Kx Q2s+ Q6o+ J2s+ J7o+ T2s+ T7o+ 94s+ 96o+ 84s+ 86o+ 74s+ 76o 63s+ 65o 53s+ 43s
Big Blind call	27.3% 44+ A2s+ A3o+ K6s+ K9o+ Q9s+ Qto+ JTs

PKO final table Blind vs Blind ranges	
Small Blind shove	41.4% 22+ Ax K2s+ K4o+ Q5s+ Q9o+ J7s+ J9o+ T7s+ 97s+ 87s
Big Blind call	40.5% 22+ Ax K2s+ K5o+ Q5s+ Q9o+ J7s+ J9o+ T7s+ 97s+ 87s 76s

It shouldn't surprise you that the Small Blind pushes wide in every situation and the Big Blind calls relatively wide. In all examples the maxim of needing a better hand to call a bet than to make a bet applies. In the normal final table example we see a bigger divergence between the shoving and calling range than in the ChipEV example, because of the impact of ICM.

What is noteworthy in both PKO examples is that the shoving and calling ranges are almost identical to each other. The hands you would push as the Small Blind are essentially the hands you would call as the Big Blind, even when ICM is a factor. This, once again, highlights the fact that the upside of calling and winning is so much greater than the downside of calling and losing when the bounties are a factor. As the Big Blind when you call and win you take the bounty, have a better chance at winning the remaining bounties and move up a pay jump.

This is obviously important to understand when you cover people at a final table but just as important to be aware of when you are covered with a big bounty on your head. There are going to be a lot of spots at a PKO final table where you have no fold equity whatsoever if your opponents understand the format. You need to push with hands that figure to be ahead of a wide calling range.

PKOs and ICM - A summary

We chose a single example to cover all hands where ICM is a factor because we were concerned that had we gone in the other direction, and used a wide range of examples, the information might have been misapplied in a cookie cutter fashion. We didn't want to give an example where UTG limps, the Hijack isolates and we are the Big Blind, then have the reader think we were giving a blueprint to play the same way in similar looking situations, because a small change in the bounties, stack sizes and payouts would lead to an entirely different GTO answer. Instead we picked a relatively simple and standard example that covers how dramatically ICM pulls us in one direction and the bounties in the other.

What is the best way to approach the payout stages in a PKO?

Before you do a deep-dive into studying ICM influenced spots in PKOs, it's important to first get the fundamentals of tournament play right. You need to know what your ranges would be in standard tournament payout and final table spots. Only after you know what you would do in a normal tournament can you begin to factor in how the bounties adjust your range.

Just as we suggested you study your equity against standard ranges before applying the bounty discount, do the same for ICM spots. Learn what your ranges should be in a normal tournament final table or bubble, then apply the same bounty discount.

Assuming you have those fundamentals down, when you find yourself deep in a tournament, think about what your standard range would be in a hand, then ask yourself how much the bounty is expanding your range and how much the payouts are contracting it? This will be a little bit of art and science, in the moment you are going to have to make approximations, which you can then study in detail later. You'll find you get better at this over time.

The heads-up stage

This is perhaps the best place to make a quick observation about the heads-up stage of a PKO. There are literally no strategy adjustments in a PKO tournament compared to a normal MTT when it gets to the heads-up stage. There is no longer ICM because it is now winner-takes-all. The bounties should not change your ranges anymore either because now, like in a regular MTT, you are just competing for the remainder of the prize pool. So don't do anything differently, but a few things you should be aware of.

First of all, acknowledge you are not playing for the bounties anymore, just the remaining prize pool. Let's say 2nd gets $1,000, 1st gets $2,000, you have a $500 bounty on your head and your opponent has a $750 bounty on theirs. Just think of this as a regular heads-up match where 2nd gets $1,000 and 1st gets $3,250 (or the remaining $2,250). Your strategic decisions are no different to any other heads-up match.

However, while you understand this, your opponent might not. They still might be calling wider than they should because they think they should be going nuts for bounties; you might have to adjust your range accordingly.

Finally, it is useful to know how top-heavy PKO tournaments tend to be. Most of the time you will be playing for a bigger prize heads-up than in the equivalent normal MTT. When you are heads-up in a PKO you are playing for a portion of every bounty that has been won, your own bounty and the regular payout top prize.

It's for this reason that after studying your equity against standard ranges as well as the Bounty Discounts, the next best thing to do in your poker study is to get solid at heads-up. The few times you get heads-up in a PKO it is important for your bottom line that you actually win it. Operators are realising this and at the time of writing many have changed the standard payouts so that 1st and 2nd get the same standard prize, so the difference between 1st and 2nd is the bounties. So in the example above, 1st and 2nd would get $1,500 each and compete for the remaining $1,250 in bounties, essentially meaning 1st gets $2,750 and 2nd gets $1,500.

Key takeaways

- When ICM is a factor, think about what your standard range would be in a hand then ask yourself how much the bounty is expanding your range and how much ICM is contracting it
- In your study, work on developing a good understanding of your standard ranges in a normal MTT first as a foundation for studying PKO spots
- Often you will have no fold equity at all as the short stack at a PKO final table
- The heads-up stage is not influenced by ICM or bounties, so play it like a normal MTT

Chapter 8. Shoves

Now that we have looked at ICM we hope you agree that showcasing the differences between four spots is the better way to approach those situations than trying to provide a complete blueprint for playing in the payout stages. By the same token we think highlighting the differences between spots is the best way to approach our next section, shoves.

It's common to get short stacked in any form of tournament and when you get to around 15 big blinds or less, your only strategy most of the time is to shove or fold. The reason why we have waited until after the ICM chapter to discuss PKO shoving ranges is that ICM has a dramatic effect on shoving ranges in general, so we want to compare ICM influenced spots to early spots in the same way as the last chapter.

Even when you are short stacked, ICM pressure means you have fold equity, which is why a shove/fold strategy as a short stack is effective in tournaments. Your opponents will fold hands they know are ahead of your shoving range if calling and losing would hurt their chances of a big payout, and they would be correct to do this a lot of the time. This came into sharp focus in our previous book *Poker Satellite Strategy* where we highlighted some spots where it is correct to shove 100% of your range, because your opponent would be correct to fold Pocket Aces preflop.

How does the fact we are playing in a PKO influence our shoving ranges when our opponents are incentivised to call us to win a bounty? We have already seen how wide we should be calling in a PKO after applying the Bounty Discount, so with that in mind how should our shoving ranges change when we are short stacked?

As you can imagine, the answer to this question is incredibly complex and situation dependent. If we are short at a final table with one starting bounty and everyone covers us, the range will be one extreme, if we are short with five starting bounties in the middle stages it will be another. If we are shoving and one player behind us is shorter than us, thus we can win their bounty, the range changes once again. We've also seen crazy simulations where if everyone was short enough with equal stacks and big bounties it would be correct for everyone at the table to go all-in.

PKOs are just so complex that it is not practical to try and replicate every situation. Once again we are going to look at the same situation in four different formats to ascertain the differences between situations.

In each example we are looking at a nine handed table where everyone has 12 big blinds except for the Hero, who has 10 big blinds. This means in the PKO examples, we cannot win a bounty but our opponents can. The examples are once again normal ChipEV/early in an MTT, early in a PKO where everyone has the starting bounty, at a normal final table of a 90man PokerStars SNG and at a PKO final table with the same relative payout structure where everyone has the average bounty. One difference this time is we are going to move the short stack, so we are going to look at the ranges UTG, MP2 and Button.

These are the ranges for UTG in each scenario.

UTG 10 big blind shoving range	
Format	*Range*
ChipEV	16.0% 33+ A7s+ A5–A4s ATo+ K9s+ KQo+ Q9s+ J9s+ T9s
Early PKO	14.6% 44+ A7s+ A5s ATo+ K9s+ KJo QTs+ J9s+ T9s
Normal Final Table	15.1% 55+ A2s+ ATo+ KTs+ KJo+ QTs+
PKO Final Table	11.9% 88+ 66 A2s+ AJo+ KTs+ KQo QJs

Before we look at the PKO examples, let's compare ChipEV to a normal final table. The frequency of the ranges are very close, 16.0% to 15.1%, but the shape of the ranges are quite different. ChipEV includes most pairs, most of the suited broadway hands and the better Aces. The normal final table, however, has two less pairs, less suited broadway, but all the suited Aces.

The reason for this change in the shape of the range is a direct response to the type of hands that would be calling in a GTO world. If it was folded to the Big Blind they could call with 44+ A5s+ A9o+ KTs+ KQo QJs in the ChipEV example and in the final table example they could call with 99+ AQ+. The shoving hands in the ChipEV example have good equity when called against the Big Blind's range, the small pairs and suited broadway hands do well against a calling range that includes similar hands. The shoving hands in the final table example have good equity when called against that tighter range, but more importantly they have blockers. We can shove all the suited Aces in that range because having an Ace in our hand limits the number of combinations of hands that can call us. If the Big Blind can only call with 99+ and AQ+ then we will get more folds because we make them having AA, AK or AQ less likely, and when we are called we often have a suited Ace that can get us out of trouble.

The value of blockers in our shoving range should not be understated and you will see how powerful they are as we go on.

Now let's look at how the ranges change in PKOs. First of all, early in a PKO, the difference is relatively minor. We have to tighten up a little. We can only shove with 14.6% of our hands compared to around 16% of hands in the other examples. This should make sense, we have less fold equity this early in a PKO when winning that bounty is huge for the rest of the table.

Finally, if you look at the PKO final table you can see something similar to what happened between the two non-PKO examples we looked at. The frequency is similar, we can shove a few more hands and we can shove all our suited Aces, compared to A9s+ in the early PKO example. We also lose some of the worst suited broadway hands and the worst pair. Again, this change in the shape of the range is a function of the GTO calling ranges (if it was folded around to the Big Blind they could call with 55+ A8s+ ATo+ KJs+ KQo) and in particular the blocker effect of having an Ace in our hand.

One final fun note for that range is you will notice that 66 is a shove but 77 is not. This came up in our satellite book too and it is not a mistake. 66 has slightly better equity than 77 against a tight calling range that includes a lot of Ax hands, specifically because on a 2345x runout it makes a better straight than the wheel made by Ax.

Looking at these side by side comparisons, it is clear the biggest factor at play is the ability to win bounties. When you cannot win a bounty, your shoving range needs to tighten up considerably. ICM does influence your shoving range late on in PKOs and you can expect some folds, but for the most part weights your range to strong hands that have good equity when called. Before we go any further, this should help to dismiss a belief a lot of players have that when they get short in PKOs they should gamble for a big stack. As is often the case in poker, it helps to do the opposite of what your opponents are doing, so in this case tighten up when they are calling wide.

That is just one example, however, so let's look at the same spot but move the short stack to MP2. This is what their shoving range would be in each format:

MP2 shoving range	
Format	*Range*
ChipEV	25.1% 22+ A2s+ A7o+ A5o K8s+ KTo+ Q9s+ QJo J8s+ T8s 98s 87s
Early PKO	23.3% 22+ A2s+ A7o+ A5o K9s+ KTo+ Q9s+ QJo J9s+ T9s 98s
Normal Final Table	24.7% 22+ A2s+ A9o+ A5o–A4o K4s+ KTo+ Q9s+ QTo+ J9s+ T9s
PKO Final Table	21.1% 22+ A2s+ ATo+ K6s+ KTo+ Q9s+ QJo J9s+ T9s

Unsurprising that every example has a wider shoving range, for the simple reason that the Hero has fewer players to get through, so their shoves will take it down more often. They also can expect to get called a bit wider in each scenario, so a wider shoving range will perform better against a wider calling range.

The early PKO range is still heavily weighted towards suited high cards that will perform well against a wide calling range, it still doesn't include every Ace. The PKO final table range has added more suited Kings to expand the blocker effect of the suited Aces, but still doesn't include all the Aces.

If you look at the shapes of the ranges, the early PKO range is actually a very similar shape to ChipEV, just with the bottom shaved off. The same goes for the normal final table and the PKO final table, which are both weighted towards suited Aces and suited Kings. The lesson here appears to be that ICM status is a more useful metric to compare two ranges than bounty status. If you are at a PKO final table think of your normal final table ranges, then expand on those, rather than your early PKO ranges.

Finally, let's look at the ranges for if the Button was the short stack.

Button shoving range	
Format	*Range*
ChipEV	45.3% 22+ Ax K2s+ K5o+ Q4s+ Q9o+ J6s+ J9o+ T6s+ T9o 96s+ 86s+ 75s+ 65s 54s
Early PKO	41.8% 22+ Ax K2s+ K5o+ Q5s+ Q9o+ J7s+ J9o T7s+ T9o 97s 87s 76s
Normal Final Table	53.9% 22+ Ax K2s+ K5o+ Q2s+ Q8o+ J2s+ J8o+ T3s+ T8o+ 95s+ 97o+ 85s+ 87o+ 74s+ 64s+ 53s+ 43s
PKO Final Table	43.9% 22+ Ax K2s+ K8o+ Q3s+ Q9o+ J5s+ J9o+ T6s+ T8o+ 96s+ 98o 85s+ 75s+ 65s 54s

The later you get in position, the wider you can shove and, from an ICM perspective, the closer your frequencies fall in line with ChipEV. You can shove super wide at a normal final table with only two players to get through and ICM pressure on them. The same is true at a PKO final table, where it might surprise you to learn a short stack can profitably shove 54s against the blinds.

Comparing ChipEV to early PKO, the worst suited connectors drop out of the PKO range, because the blinds are still heavily incentivised to call in non-ICM scenarios. So the Button's range early in a PKO is still weighted towards high cards that should be ahead when called a lot of the time.

One interesting observation is that the later you get, the frequency of the PKO final table gets closer to the frequency of ChipEV. The two ranges for the Button are very similar to each other as you get to late position. This is a good example of the midway point on the ICM dial, where we see the effect of the bounty and ICM cancelling each other out, bringing us back to normal ChipEV.

We have looked at three spots in four different ways to get an idea of how early PKO and ICM PKO scenarios change our range. There are so many factors which you will discover change the ranges again in your self-study, including the size of the bounty and the presence of shorter stacks at the table. One big final factor to consider is the tendencies of the players at your table. These ranges are GTO shoving ranges assuming your opponent's know what they should be calling with. You will discover that some players will call regardless of the ICM pressure and that will change your ranges even more, and some players simply do not know what it means to be in a PKO and you will get folds you never expected.

Now we have looked at open shoves, let's take a look at how wide we can shove over the opening bet of another player.

Key Takeaways

- When you are short early in a PKO you should tighten up your shoving ranges because you will get called
- You will get some folds in ICM PKO spots, so adjust your range to include blockers, but keep it tighter than normal ICM spots
- It's more practical to compare PKO ranges to their relative normal MTT range, than it is to compare early PKO spots to ICM PKO spots

Chapter 9. 3-betting

We have looked at shoving ranges, what about 3-betting ranges in PKOs?

The example we have decided to use to cover 3-betting is the same one from the ICM chapter, but we have changed the stacks. It is folded round to the Button at a table full of medium stacks, the Button has 60 big blinds, the Small Blind has 12 big blinds and the Big Blind has 40 big blinds.

The Button min raises to two big blinds and we are looking at the 3-betting range of the Small Blind as well as the 4-betting range of the Big Blind. Then, of course, we are looking at the calling range of the Button against both reraises. This is an example that does a lot because both players have to worry about the Big Blind, which should have a contracting influence on the ranges in general, but perhaps not so much with two bounties involved.

Once again, we are looking at the same spot at a ChipEV, early PKO, normal final table and PKO final table hand. The early PKO has not had any eliminations yet and the PKO final table assumes everyone has an average bounty. This is using the PokerStars 90 man SNG payout structure. The ranges have been calculated using Hold'em Resources Calculator.

The table make up looks like this:

30k starting stack
250/500 level

UTG: 50,000
UTG+1: 50,000
MP1: 50,000
MP2: 50,000
MP3: 50,000
CO: 50,000

BTN: *30,000*
SB: *6,000*
BB: *20,000*

Let's begin by looking at the min raising range of the Button.

Button opening range	
Format	*Range*
ChipEV	49.5% 22+ Kx Q6s+ Q7o+ J7s+ J7o+ T8s+ T8o+ 97s+ 87s
Early PKO	71.4% 22+ Kx Q2s+ Q3o+ J2s+ J7o+ T2s+ T6o+ 92s+ 96o+ 84s+ 86o+ 73s+ 76o 63s+ 65o 52s+ 54o
Normal Final Table	53.2% 22+ Kx Q7s+ Q2s Q6o+ J6s+ J6o+ T6s+ T6o+ 98s
PKO Final Table	56.1% 22+ Kx Q2s+ Q8o+ J8o+ J6s J4s–J3s T8s+ T7o+ T5o 98s 87s

Not a great deal of difference between the ChipEV, normal final table or PKO final table ranges in this example, less than 7% between them. The Button can open very wide because they only have two players to get through, they have their opponents covered and they have position if they get called. The normal final table is a bit wider than ChipEV because of ICM pressure on the other two players, the PKO final table a bit wider than that for the same reason, plus the bounties.

The most interesting example here is the early PKO spot, which is a whopping 71.4% of hands that can be played by the Button. This includes hands as weak as 52s+ and 54o. The reason for this massive expansion of the ranges is because the bounties mean so much more relatively in the early stages of a PKO compared to the payout stages. Because we can win two of them and when we do we cover the rest of the table in future hands, our range is super wide. ICM is pulling the Button in the other direction quite a lot in the PKO final table example by comparison, and we see the really speculative hands drop out of the range.

Now we know what we can open, what hands should the Small Blind be 3-betting all-in with against that range?

Small Blind reshoving range	
Format	*Range*
ChipEV	33.6% 22+ Ax K3s+ K8o+ Q8s+ QTo+ J8s+ JTo+ T8s+ 98s
Early PKO	40.4% 22+ Ax K2s+ K5o+ Q5s+ Q8o+ J8s+ J9o+ T8s+ 98s
Normal Final Table	33.8% 22+ Ax K4s+ K9o+ Q8s+ QTo+ J8s+ JTo T7s+ 97s+ 87s 76s
PKO Final Table	31.2% 22+ Ax K5s+ K9o+ Q8s+ QTo+ J9s+ JTo T9s 98s

Like in the previous example the difference between ChipEV, normal final table and PKO final table is hardly noticeable. The ranges are virtually the same in each spot.

What will probably surprise you is in the early PKO example, the reshoving range of the Small Blind is higher than the other three examples. It is 40.4% of hands compared to the next highest of 33.8%. This might go against your intuition because of what we have explored so far, after all, the Small Blind is the shortest stack at the table and the Button and Big Blind are highly incentivised to call them for the bounty.

The reason why this range is the widest of all is that the Button's opening range is so wide. This presents the Small Blind with their best chance of doubling up. When the Button can open 71.4% of hands, the Small Blind can reshove profitably with 40.4% of hands.

The reason why the other three examples are all around the 32% range is that the respective opening ranges are all around 53%. How wide you can 3-bet profitably has a direct correlation with how wide your opponent is opening.

The interesting take away from both the Button and Small Blind ranges in the early PKO is the type of hands each player adds to their range. The Button is adding a lot of suited connecting hands, the Small Blind is adding mostly high cards. When they know they are getting called wide the Small Blind wants hands that hold up without improvement (even 98s could, in theory, be ahead against the Button). The Button doesn't mind being behind because the bounty increases their upside, and suitedness puts a cap on how far they can be behind against most hands.

Given that the Small Blind is expecting to get called a lot, let's look at what the Button can call the reshove with, assuming the Big Blind gets out of the way.

Button calling range	
Format	*Range*
ChipEV	36.7% 22+ Ax K2s+ K7o+ Q6s+ Q9o+ J8s+ JTo T8s+ 97s+ 87s
Early PKO	71.4% 22+ Kx Q2s+ Q3o+ J2s+ J7o+ T2s+ T6o+ 92s+ 96o+ 84s+ 86o+ 73s+ 76o 63s+ 65o 52s+ 54o
Normal Final Table	30.1% 22+ Ax K5s+ K9o+ Q9s+ QTo+ J9s+ T9s 98s
PKO Final Table	32.7% 22+ Ax K4s+ K9o+ Q8s+ QTo+ J8s+ JTo T8s+ 98s 87s

The ChipEV, normal final table and PKO final table ranges again are virtually the same and consistent with the reshoving ranges of the

Small Blind. In fact they are virtually the same percentages as the reshoving ranges.

What may have hit you right away is that the Button's calling range in the early PKO example is that it has not changed. We open 71.4% of hands and we call 71.4% of hands against the Small Blind when they reshove. This is an example where the Small Blind literally has no fold equity, but that doesn't matter because the Small Blind has crafted a range designed to double up against the Button. When a smaller stack has a bounty worth winning, the Button is only playing hands they are happy to call an all-in with.

This is a very important lesson, and worth noting: There are some spots in a PKO where you are only looking to win the bounty, so you shouldn't play any hands you are going to bet/fold. Likewise, there are times when as the covered player you have zero fold equity, so your range should be weighted towards hands that can double up without improvement.

This equilibrium is clearly understood between the Button and the Small Blind, but what about that pesky Big Blind? What happens when they get involved? First of all, what hands should they be 4-betting all-in with when the Button opens and the Small Blind reshoves?

Big Blind 4-betting range	
Format	Range
ChipEV	14.3% 44+ A7s+ A5s A9o+ KTs+ KQo QJs
Early PKO	32% 22+ Ax K5s+ K9o+ Q8s+ QTo+ J9s+ JTo T8s+ 98s 87s
Normal Final Table	11.7% 55+ A7s+ A9o+ KJs+
PKO Final Table	12.8% 44+ A7s+ A9o+ KJs+ KQo

Again, no big difference between ChipEV, normal final table and PKO final table. They all require around 13% of the top hands to get it in. Against two opponents, one of whom has committed all their chips, we need a strong hand even if the ranges before us were wide. We have to win the hand at showdown against the Small Blind and if the Button does call we have to beat two likely strong hands, so our hand has to be strong too.

In the early PKO we can shove much wider by comparison, 32% of hands. We cover the Small Blind so we can win a bounty, but we cannot go nuts and call any two because the Button covers us and will be incentivised to call. We know the Small Blind is weighted towards high cards and the Button has added a lot of small suited cards to their range, the shape of our range reflects that. It is still high card heavy but also includes the better half of the suited cards, hands like J9s and 87s are also in there. It's the middle ground between the two adjusted ranges of our opponents, we need the high cards to match the range of the Small Blind, we need the suited cards to help us out if we get called by the Button.

Finally, let's look at how wide the Button can call when they are facing a shove and a reshove. Remember we could call with 71.4% of hands in the early PKO example when the Big Blind folded.

Button calling both Small and Big Blind	
Format	*Range*
ChipEV	8% 66+ ATs+ AJo+
Early PKO	32.7% 22+ Ax K4s+ K9o+ Q8s+ QTo+ J9s+ JTo+ T8s+ 98s 87s
Normal Final Table	4.2% 99+ AQs+ AKo
PKO Final Table	4.7% 88+ AQs+ AKo

In the other three scenarios the Button is now forced to call with just the top end of their range, though it is notable that ChipEV is significantly wider (8%) than PKO final table (4.7%) or normal final table (4.2%), relatively. This is the ICM pressure in the driving seat, against two opponents all-in you need the best hand, even with bounties at a final table.

The difference between those three and an early PKO is profound. We can call 32% of hands in this spot. We throw away the complete junk like 52s and keep all the broadway hands, pairs and better suited connectors like 98s and J9s. Again, we need that middle ground of high cards that could be ahead and suitedness that could get us out of trouble when behind.

Perhaps the most interesting thing of all is that our range is almost identical to the Big Blind's 4-betting range. We've seen this before and it is unique to PKOs, that the calling range just has to match the shoving range.

In this hand example we have seen remarkable consistency between the ChipEV, normal final table and PKO final table examples. This does not mean that the same will hold true in other 3-betting and 4-betting examples you will encounter. Throw in a particularly big bounty at the PKO final table or a micro stack who has folded under-the-gun in the normal final table example, and the ranges will diverge dramatically. Likewise, when the player who is 3-betting covers the opener, you'll discover the ranges change once again. By now you know we are just looking at the differences between the ranges to make some broader points.

The big lesson here is that early on in a PKO we are heavily incentivised to go for the bounties and as such, as the coverer we can min raise a wide range with the intention of calling a reshove a lot of the time. Likewise, when we are covered, we should be aware of how little fold equity we have and adjust our range for hands we think will double us up. 3-betting is profitable in other formats in part because they allow our opponents to fold, we cannot bank on that in a PKO and it is not a bad thing, but we should adjust our ranges accordingly.

Key Takeaways

- How wide you can reshove profitably correlates with how wide your opponent opens
- Don't expect anyone to fold to your reshoves, instead adjust your range to include high cards and pairs that will likely win against a wide range
- There are a lot of situations in early PKOs where if you open a hand as the coverer, you should be prepared to call a shove with it

Chapter 10. Post flop

Other than giving a brief mention to the fact that the Bounty Discount calculation works exactly the same post flop as it does preflop, we have somewhat steered away from any discussion of post flop poker. This is because this book is mainly about covering the key adjustments you need to make in PKOs, and preflop examples are a much easier way to get them across. It is also because PKOs are quite skewed towards being a preflop game, especially at the lower stakes. Barry has commented to me that he considers himself a good satellite and PKO player, but a bad regular MTT player, because PKOs and satellites mask a lot of his post flop leaks, and there is a broader element of truth to that observation.

Now that you have hopefully ingrained the key adjustments, we did want to touch on a few considerations pertaining to post flop play, which is best explained with the following example.

The effective stacks are 5,000 which is also the starting stack. Blinds are 200/400 with a 25 ante and we are eight-handed. UTG is a very tight player and when they open to 800, we put them on a very tight range of 99+ AQ+. We look down at 89o in the Big Blind and we call.

There is 2,000 in the pot. The flop is A-7-6 rainbow.

We check, they bet 1,000 and we shove for 4,200.

How profitable is this play?

If we get called, we are always behind and we are always drawing to our straight only, because UTG always has an Ace or an overpair to any top pair we can make. So if he always calls, we have 33% equity.

If he always calls, we are shoving 4,200 to win a pot of 10,000.

Our share of the pot is 33%, or 3,300. So this 4,200 bet is actually a -900 play (4,200-3,300). A bad idea.

But what if they fold some of the time? Let's say they fold 25% of the time with hands like 99-JJ.

When UTG folds, we win the 3,000 that was in the pot 25% of the time, our expectation would be 750 (25% of 3,000).

25% of the time we win 750 and 75% of the time we lose 900, on average.

75% of -900 is -675 plus the 750 we win 25% of the time. -675 + 750 = 75.

Assuming UTG does fold sometimes, this actually gives this play an expectation of +75. This is a winning play, even though when we get called we have the worst of it.

This is why semi bluffing is a powerful tool in a regular MTT, we make money by denying equity to our opponent but we have something in our back pocket for when we get called.

Now let's look at the same situation in a PKO. Exactly the same spot, but we cover UTG who has a starting bounty.

Effective stacks 5,000 which is also the starting stack, we cover UTG who has a starting bounty
UTG opens (99+ AQ+) to 800
We defend BB: 89o
2k in pot
Flop: A-7-6 rainbow
We check, he bets 1,000, we shove 4,200
How profitable is this play?

For the purposes of illustration we will use a more widely adopted calculation in PKOs called the Chip Conversion Model. This is where the value of the bounty is added to the calculation as if it were extra chips in the pot. A starting bounty is worth ⅓ of a starting stack worth of chips, which you treat like it is dead money in the pot. Our Bounty Discount model is the easier method to use for preflop spots, but we think the Chip Conversion Model is more useful for post flop spots.

If we assume UTG never folds, then in chip terms once again we will win 33% of the time in a 10,000 pot, so our 4,200 bet is worth 3,300 chips.

However, this is a PKO and that starting bounty is worth ⅓ of a starting stack, so in this example an extra 1,666 in the pot.

In addition to our 3,300 share of the pot, we would win another 1,666 in the form of a realised bounty. We add that to the -900 and it actually gives us a positive expectation of +766.

This means it is more profitable for us to get our bet called when we are a ChipEV underdog than it is for us to get our opponent to fold. Our expectation is +966 when we are always called in a PKO but it is +75 when we can make our opponent fold some of the time in the first example. In a normal MTT we like taking our semi bluffs down without a fight, but in a PKO we prefer being called because getting the bounty makes being an equity underdog worth it.

The takeaway here is that in a PKO there are a lot of spots where you are actually rooting for your opponent to call even when you are most likely to lose the hand.

How should this affect your play? In a normal MTT we like to have fold equity for the reasons given, but in a PKO the more profitable line is often to pot commit your opponent, even when they have a made hand. The worst thing you could do is call them on the turn, hit your hand then give them a chance to fold when that obvious scare card hits. Much better sometimes to check raise them on the flop if they already have put quite a lot in to try and get the rest committed.

One final note on playing draws in PKOs is that another reason to play draws aggressively is that you might get your money in ahead without having to improve. This is actually quite a common occurrence in PKOs, let's say the flop is 2-9-T rainbow. You could check raise all-in with QJo and actually get called by 78o for a worse draw. Even better, you could have KJo on the same flop for a gutshot, get your money in the middle and get called by QJo. In this spot the QJo is the better draw, but you have the better hand and you also block the straight getting there with your King. You would prefer the QJo in this spot in a regular MTT where you would only ever get called by a made hand so you need to improve, but KJo is a 72% favourite against QJo and these are spots that come up often in PKOs.

Dry flops

We play draws aggressively and like to get called with them in PKOs because our equity is more important in this format than simply having the best hand right now. What about when we have the made hand and/or the flop is dry?

I like to look down at my hand and ask myself "is this the sort of hand that could stack somebody?" – in other words, can I hit the flop hard enough to get my opponent to commit all their chips with a worse hand? Small pairs and suited connectors are obvious examples of this, but we cannot really say the same when we have A6o and the flop comes A73 rainbow. This is the sort of flop where if we get action, we are way behind, as we probably only get looked up by better Aces and sets.

Post flop there are a lot of spots where we are going to be very happy getting our money in with bottom pair and a gutshot, but we have to tread very carefully with top pair, no kicker. Ironically, in a game where we can massively expand our 'get in' range, often top pair type hands work much better playing for pot control, bluff catching and generally winning small pots. You might even have to find some folds with top pair where you never would with bottom pair and a draw.

Ask yourself on the flop "is it realistic to get all of their stack here if they have a worse hand?" and if the answer is no, it is probably better to adopt a standard MTT strategy.

Bet sizing

One final thing to think about post flop is your bet sizing. As we have seen, a good general principle is to keep the players in whom you cover. With this in mind, if somebody bets the flop and you have a strong hand, if another player who you cover is left to act, now might be a good time to call. This goes double if you have a hand strong enough to call a squeeze as you will often be getting the right price to do so. If there isn't a player left to act whom you cover, now you can instead look to trying to get the money in by reraising.

If you cover a single opponent, you should be looking for ways to increase your bet sizing if necessary to make it more likely you can win the bounty. Manipulate the pot in such a way that you can make a stack sized river bet. When I play a normal MTT my bet sizing is determined by the flop type. If I have range advantage and/or it's a dry flop I tend to bet small because those pots are easier to take down. If there are lots of draws I bet bigger because I can get more value and charge people the wrong price to outdraw me.

In a PKO my bet sizing is based entirely on my opponent's stack when I cover them. PKOs are about stack manipulation, not pot manipulation. If I do cover them I aim to bet 10% of their stack on the flop (not a percentage of the pot), because by doing that I can bet ⅔ of the pot on the turn and as such it means my river shove will not be an overbet.

For example, let's say they have a 10,000 stack and there is 2,000 in the middle of the table post flop.

If I bet 1,000 on the flop and they call, I can bet 2,640 on the turn into a 4,000 pot, if they call that then I can bet 6,360 on the river which would set them all in and it would be well under a pot sized bet into the 9,280 pot.

It will be much easier for my opponent to call on the river when I am not overbetting because I'll be giving them a good price to do so. The problem with overbets is that they allow people more room to fold and they also are quite a clear bet sizing tell, you are literally spelling out that you have a good enough hand to win a bounty.

Preflop in PKOs is already such a complex beast that it will never be truly solved and post flop the unanswered questions are infinite. It's beyond the remit of this book to go much further with post flop considerations without completely overwhelming you (and ourselves). Until you feel you have the preflop fundamentals down, keep the post flop analysis on the back burner a little, but do commit to studying specific hands in the future with like-minded players, using post flop solvers and equity calculators.

Key takeaways

- Playing draws aggressively when you can win a bounty is almost always profitable even if you think you will be called 100% of the time
- Weak top pair hands are not necessarily automatic 'get ins'
- In general bet bigger when you can win a bounty
- If you bet 10% of your opponent's stack on the flop, then bet 2/3rds pot on the turn, you can set them all-in on the river for less than the size of the pot

- PKOs post flop are about stack manipulation, not pot manipulation

Chapter 11. Opening ranges

We have covered the biggest decisions you will make such as when to call shoves, when to shove and ICM decisions. Now let's look at a smaller, but still important, consideration - when to open hands. This might seem odd to have near the end of the book but, as already stated, we have assumed you are a seasoned player and we thought it was better to write chapters in order of the biggest adjustments. Min raising is a small factor compared to ICM spots or calling all-ins, but there are some things unique about PKOs which should change your approach.

We have picked out two different scenarios, both very different from each other, which teach us a lot about how opening ranges change in PKOs.

One quick note for anyone proficient in post flop solver technology. These ranges have been calculated using Holdem Resources Calculator which is a preflop solver and it recommends some hands as opens (instead of shoves) in part because of their EV post flop. HRC is very powerful but is flawed assessing the post flop equity realisation of some hands compared to post flop solvers like PIOSolver. We are presenting the following splits purely to give you a baseline for how much the PKO solution differs from the non-PKO. If you want to see a more accurate solution to spots like this, we recommend Michael Acevedo's book *Modern Poker Theory* which provides a preflop framework that takes post flop equity realisation into account.

20 big blinds effective

Let's begin with some examples when there are 20 big blinds effective in a pot, because here the big decision is not just about whether we should play our hand, but whether we should min raise or shove? In normal MTTs it would be typical to split our range between folds, min raises and shoves. The shoves are usually hands that have good equity but do not play well post flop (like small pairs), the min raises are usually a mix of very strong hands and hands that realise their equity well post flop (like suited broadway hands). There will also be hands we are prepared to bet/fold.

How does this change in a PKO?

In the next few examples the table makeup will be like this, and the only changes will be on the Button, Small Blind and Big Blind.

UTG 72 big blinds
UTG+1 20 big blinds
MP1 30 big blinds
MP2 30 big blinds
MP3 8 big blinds
CO 10 big blinds
BU 40 big blinds
SB 20 big blinds
BB 20 big blinds

In this first example it is folded around to the Button who has 40 big blinds, while the Small Blind and Big Blind both have 20 big blinds. This is a non-ICM normal MTT example:

Early on normal MTT no PKO	
Position	*Range*
Button Min Raise	5.3% KK+ A2o KTo–K8o Q9o
Button Shove	29.8% QQ–22 A2s+ A3o+ K5s+ KJo+ Q8s+ QTo+ J8s+ JTo T7s+ 97s+ 87s 76s 65s

As you can see the solver technology we used advocates a mix of min raising and shoving, mostly shoving. We min raise a mix of the strongest hands and the weakest hands for the purpose of balance, we want to be able to have strong hands when we get reraised but we need enough weaker hands in there so our opponent knows we have a bet/fold range too. Most of the time, however, we shove our range because against just two opponents it will get folds a lot of the time and also get called by weaker hands.

Now let's look at the same example, but this time it is early in a PKO. Both our opponents have a Bounty Factor of 1, we have 40 big blinds, they both have 20 big blinds.

Early in a PKO	
Position	*Range*
Button Min Raise	0%
Button Shove	49.9% 22+ Ax K2s+ K5o+ Q2s+ Q8o+ J4s+ J9o+ T6s+ T8o+ 96s+ 98o 85s+ 87o 75s+ 64s+ 53s+ 43s

We can play a much wider range (almost half our hands compared to 35.2% of our hands) and we should shove our entire range. This might go against your instinct, a lot of people would assume if we are trying to win bounties we should be slowly building the pot and letting our opponents in cheaply.

If we look at what the GTO calling ranges are in this spot, it sheds some light on why shoving is the optimal approach.

Calling Ranges	
Position	*Range*
SB call	30.3% 22+ Ax K6s+ K9o+ Q8s+ QTo+ J9s+ T9s
BB call if SB folds	31.9% 22+ Ax K5s+ K8o+ Q8s+ QTo+ J9s+ JTo
BB call if SB calls	30.5% 22+ A2s+ A7o+ A5o K5s+ K9o+ Q8s+ QTo+ J8s+ JTo T7s+ 97s+ 86s+ 76s 65s

Even though we cover our opponents, because we are shoving wide, they can call wide. Both can call with just over 30% of their range, which plays well against a 50% shoving range. Note also that the Big Blind can call almost as wide if the Small Blind calls, because they can win the Small Blind's bounty.

Although the percentages are about the same, the shape of the Big Blind's range changes when the Small Blind calls. They can call with any Ace when it's against the Button, as high card hands play well against a 50% shoving range, but they throw away the weakest Aces but add hands like 65s, which play well multiway.

This same example gets really interesting when you increase the Bounty Factor of the two Blinds. This is the same example, we have 40 big blinds and our opponents have 20 big blinds, but those 20 big blinds are ⅕ of a starting stack, so they have a Bounty Factor of 5.

PKO early, we cover two players both ⅕ of starting stack	
Position	*Range*
Button Min Raise	0%
Button Shove	100% Any Two

Again, these are the calling ranges to shed some light on why we don't min raise at all:

Button shove calling ranges	
Position	*Range*
SB call	80.1% 22+ Jx T2s+ T4o+ 92s+ 95o+ 82s+ 85o+ 73s+ 75o+ 63s+ 65o 53s+ 43s
BB call if SB folds	62.5% 22+ Qx J2s+ J5o+ T4s+ T7o+ 95s+ 97o+ 86s+
BB call if SB calls	91.8% 22+ 9x 82s+ 84o+ 72s+ 74o+ 62s+ 64o+ 52s+ 53o+ 42s+ 43o 32s

The Bounty Factors are so significant that it is profitable for us to play 100% of our hands, because we have the potential to win two bounties. It is profitable for us to play 7-2 offsuit in this spot.

Once again, we can shove because our opponents can call us very wide. It's an unusual equilibrium where we can get it in wide because our upside is much greater than theirs, but they can also get it in wide because we present their best chance of doubling up.

The reason why we shove rather than min raise is that when our goal is to win the bounties, it is a cardinal sin to let our opponent fold later in the hand. The last thing we want to do is min raise, let our opponents call, then have them check/fold when they miss the flop. By shoving we ensure that we are guaranteed to get a bounty when they call us and we win.

We also included the option to limp as the Button in our simulations because there was a certain logic to limping as the big stack, because it makes it more likely the Small Blind will complete and impossible for the Big Blind to fold preflop. Plenty of players would assume that 'stringing people along' like this is an optimal play and it certainly might be a good exploit for some opponents. However, when the solver had the option to limp in these spots, it never did. Once again, with relatively shallow effective stacks, the optimal strategy is to shove because it guarantees a bounty when we get called and win.

One more very interesting thing to note is the calling ranges, look at the Small Blind's calling range compared to the Big Blind's calling range when the Small Blind folds. Do you notice anything?

It is actually wider. The Small Blind can call wider than the Big Blind when it is folded to them. You will never see this in any other format, normally the Small Blind always has to call tighter because they fear that the Big Blind will wake up with something. The Big Blind can call wider when the Small Blind folds, because they close the action. However, the reason why the Small Blind can call with 80.1% of hands compared to the 62.5% of hands the Big Blind can call with when it is folded to them, is because the Small Blind can win a bounty. They want the Big Blind to call behind them.

The Big Blind practically calls 100% of their hands when the Small Blind comes along, because they can win a bounty as well as tripling up.

In normal MTT spots where there is an all-in and a call, we want to get away unless we have an absolute monster, but these are spots where PKOs show there is usually more upside than downside. We want a three-way all-in as one of the two blinds because we get a chance to triple up, win a bounty and have a better shot at winning future bounties.

Let's look at the same spot, but this time we are at a final table and ICM is a factor. Imagine what the ranges would be at a normal non-PKO final table, if the makeup of this table has two shorter stacks who have folded ahead of the blinds (so they have significant Bubble Factors).

Normal Final Table	
Position	*Range*
Button Min Raise	11.1% QQ+ ATo-A6o KJo-K7o
Button Shove	48% JJ-22 A2s+ AJo+ A5o-A2o K2s+ KQo K6o-K3o Q2s+ Q6o+ J2s+ J7o+ T2s+ T7o+ 94s+ 97o+ 84s+ 87o 74s+ 76o 64s+ 65o 53s+ 54o 43s 32s
SB call	8.3% 77+ A9s+ AJo+ KQs
BB call if SB folds	9.9% 66+ A8s+ ATo+ KJs+

With no bounties involved, once again, we split our range between min raising and shoving, mostly shoving. We do this with a very wide range because of the ICM pressure on the blinds and the fact we only have two players to get through. Even though we are shoving wide, the blinds have to call tight because with two shorter stacks behind, busting now would be a disaster.

Now, let's look at the same spot at a PKO final table, again two shorter stacks have folded and everyone has an average bounty.

PKO Final Table	
Position	*Range*
Button Min Raise	0%
Button Shove	77.4% 22+ Ax K2s+ K3o+ Q2s+ Q4o+ J2s+ J6o+ T2s+ T6o+ 92s+ 96o+ 82s+ 85o+ 73s+ 75o+ 62s+ 65o 52s+ 54o 42s+ 32s
SB call	15.5% 66+ A5s+ A8o+ K9s+ KJo+ QJs
BB call if SB folds	5.9% 88+ AJs+ AQo+
BB call if SB calls	19.2% 55+ A3s+ A6o+ K9s+ KTo+ QTs+

When we can win bounties, the optimal way to play our range, with shallow stacks, is to shove. To guarantee the bounty when we win, we shove 100% of our range.

This time around the shove is profitable in part because of the ICM pressure, our opponents are folding a lot more

In particular, look at those calling ranges. If the Small Blind gets out of the way, the game becomes a normal tournament for the Big Blind, with no bounties to win they can only call with the top 5.9% of hands.

However, the Small Blind can call three times as wide, because they still have the potential to win the Big Blind's bounty. The Big Blind can call with 19.2% of hands when the Small Blind calls. They can call nearly four times wider when the Small Blind comes along, which would be unheard of in any other format.

One last quick experiment before we move on, we looked at the same 20 big blinds effective spot at a final table but this time it is the Button who is covered. Two shorter stacks have folded behind them meaning there was significant ICM pressure, the Button has 20 big blinds, the blinds both have 40 big blinds.

UTG 72 big blinds
UTG+1 20 big blinds
MP1 30 big blinds
MP2 30 big blinds
MP3 8 big blinds
CO 10 big blinds
BU 20 big blinds
SB 40 big blinds
BB 40 big blinds

Let's start with a non PKO example, a normal final table

Normal FT, BU covered, two short stacks at the table	
Position	*Range*
Button Min Raise	16% TT+ A9s+ ATo–A3o K9o+ QTo+
Button Shove	15.3% 99–22 A8s–A2s AJo+ K6s+ Q8s+ J8s+ JTo T8s+ 98s
SB call/3–bet	11% 66+ A9s+ ATo+ KQs
BB call if SB folds	13.2% 33+ A7s+ A9o+ KTs+ QJs

A much tighter overall range than in the previous example because we do not pose a threat to the blinds, but we can still play over 30% of our hands because of our table position. There is a relatively even split between the hands we min raise and the hands we shove. The hands we min raise are weighted towards the ones that play well post flop, whereas the shoves are ones with good raw equity but weaker equity realisation.

Now let's look at the same spot, but at a PKO final table where we are covered and, we have an average bounty.

PKO FT BU is covered, two shorter stacks at the table	
Position	*Range*
Button Min Raise	16% TT+ ATs+ A3s–A2s A8o–A4o KQs K9s–K6s KJo–K9o QTo+ JTo
Button Shove	12.7% 99–44 A9s–A4s A9o+ KJs–KTs KQo Q9s+ J8s+ T9s
SB call	8.3% 88+ ATs+ AJo+
BB call if SB folds	10.1% 55+ A9s+ ATo+ KJs+

It is a slightly tighter range, but pretty much the same thing. It's around 29% of hands with a relatively even split between min raising and folding. We can min raise a wider range of hands because we will get called wider.

This proves the rough heuristic we have adopted that when you cannot win a bounty, play as you would in a normal MTT where you assume your opponents are playing a little bit looser than usual. We shove 100% of our range when we can get a bounty, we revert back to closer to a default strategy when we cannot.

Playing as the chip leader

We could write a book just on min raising in PKOs because every situation is so unique and we actually crashed Holdem Resources Calculator doing these simulations. We have one more example which really illustrates another important concept that should help you, and that is how strategy changes as the chip leader. When you are the chip leader in a PKO you are playing for a bigger prize pool than everyone else, because right now you can win every bounty. This means you have greater upside than anyone else every single hand.

We have constructed an example which really showcases this. We are UTG and this is the table makeup. The starting stacks were 30,000.

UTG 100 big blinds
UTG+1 35 big blinds
MP1 30 big blinds
MP2 10 big blinds
MP3 6 big blinds
CO 4 big blinds
BU 25 big blinds
SB 40 big blinds
BB 20 big blinds

Let's see how the ranges change in the four common examples we have been using. In the two final table examples, everyone has three bounties and three big blinds represent a starting stack.

What is our opening range?

UTG opening ranges	
Format	*Range*
ChipEV	16.3% 55+ A4s+ A8o+ K9s+ KJo+ QTs+ JTs
Early PKO	100% Any Two
Normal Final Table	19.3% 44+ A2s+ A8o+ K9s+ KTo+ Q9s+ QJo JTs
PKO Final Table	63.2% 22+ Qx J2s+ J4o+ T2s+ T6o+ 92s+ 96o+ 82s+ 85o+ 72s+ 75o+ 62s+ 64o+ 52s+ 54o 42s+ 32s

There is a lot to unpack here. First of all, in the simulations there was an option to shove and the solver never took it. With 100 big blinds and with eight players behind, we always min raise regardless of the format and stage.

There isn't a great deal of difference in the two non-PKO examples. In both cases we cannot even open 33 because it does not realise equity well at a full table. We can open a bit wider at a final table because of ICM pressure, but we are still sticking with the top end of our range, less than 20% of hands.

In both PKO examples, we can open super wide and in an early PKO we can play 100% of hands. With no ICM pressure and some very short stacks, winning bounties becomes very profitable and we should effectively play every hand. Practically speaking, you might want to avoid getting in tough spots with 92 offsuit, but it really highlights that it's OK to make small mistakes as the chip leader because the upside is so big.

For more insight into why opening nearly all of our hands is profitable as the leader in a PKO, look at how the solver advises the rest of the table to respond if it is folded around to them after we open.

How should table respond to UTG open	
Player	Range
UTG +1 (35 big blinds)	Call 32% 33+ A2s+ A3o+ K4s+ K9o+ Q8s+ Q9o+ J8s+ JTo T8s+ 98s 87s
MP1 (30 big blinds)	Call 23% 33+ A2s+ A7o+ A5o K8s+ KTo+ Q9s+ QTo+ J9s+ T9s+
MP2 (10 big blinds)	Call 20.9% 77-44 ATs-A2s AJo-A5o K6s+ K9o+ Q9s+ QTo+ J9s+ JTo T9s Shove 6% 88+ AJs+ AQo+

MP3 (6 big blinds)	Call 23.3% 77-33 ATs-A2s AJo-A4o K5s+ K9o+ Q8s+ QTo+ J8s+ JTo T9s Shove 6% 88+ AJs+ AQo+
CO (4 big blinds)	Shove 36% 22+ Ax K5s+ K9o+ Q8s+ QTo+ J9s+ JTo T9s
BU (25 big blinds)	Call 31.3% 55-33 A9s-A2s A9o-A2o KTs-K2s K6o+ Q4s+ Q8o+ J7s+ J9o+ T7s+ T9o+ 97s+ Shove 10% 66+ 22 AT+ KJs+
SB (40 big blinds)	Call 65.9% TT-33 AJs A7s-A2s AQo A8o-A2o Kx-Qx J7s+ J9o+ T8s+ T9o 92s+ 96o+ 82s+ 84o+ 73s+ 74o+ 62s+ 64o+ 52s+ 54o+ 42s+ 43o 32s 3-bet 8.9% JJ+ 22 AQs+ ATs-A8s AKo AJo-A9o
BB (20 big blinds)	Call 90.1% 44-22 A9s-A2s ATo-A2o KJs-K2s Qx-3x Shove 9.9% 55+ ATs+ AJo+ KQs

While plenty of players can reraise or shove on our opening bet, it is a small percentage of the combined range of hands that can play against us. Most players are better off flatting against us because it makes it more likely they can get a bounty by getting another player to stay in the pot. The shortest stack has all shoves in their range because the chip leader is their best chance to double up, but even the players with just ten and six big blinds are advised to call most of the time because they have a shorter player left to act behind them. Winning their bounty is huge, so even though it goes against all instincts in tournament poker, flatting is the way to go here.

The ten and six big blind stacks have the exact same shoving range, which is 88+ AJs+ AQo+. This is pretty much the default top 6% of hands we can comfortably 3-bet and not mind getting called by a strong hand. This is a pretty decent range to memorise when you know you have zero fold equity with a lot of players left to act.

If UTG was opening very wide in a normal tournament they would get exploited, the rest of the table would adapt by 3-betting them a lot, forcing them to fold or call with the worst of it. In a PKO, however, the players acting behind have to call if they want a realistic chance of getting a bounty, which means a chip leader can open with impunity.

Likewise, in a regular MTT we would worry about flatting the opening bet so wide because a savvy player could squeeze and take us both off the hand. Again, this is not really the case in a PKO in this spot. The more players in the pot the more bounties to be won, so you are more likely to see more players call to see a flop, and you also get a certain amount of protection from the chip leader, who will call a squeeze most of the time. You can see this by virtue of the fact that UTG+1 can call wider than MP1, which would not be the case in a regular MTT. UTG+1 has a lot of players covered, so they have more reasons to call than MP1, in a normal tournament MP1 would have a wider range because there are fewer players left to act behind them. Interestingly MP2 has a wider overall range than MP1 for a different reason, which is that as one of the shorter stacks there is less ICM pressure on them. -

The Cutoff, the shortest stack with just 4 big blinds, shoves their entire range of 22+ Ax K5s+ K9o+ Q8s+ QTo+ J9s+ JTo T9s. It's a pretty wide range which is a nice mix of high cards and suited connecting cards that play well in family pots. That's because short stacks we can expect a lot of calls behind. This is the calling range for the rest of the table when the Cutoff shoves:

BU (25 big blinds)	Call 15.8% 33+ A7s+ A9o+ KTs+ KJo+ QTs+ JTs
SB (40 big blinds)	Call 15.4% JJ+ 22 A7s-A2s A9o-A7o+ KTs-K5s KTo+ QTs-Q8s QTo+ J9s-J8s JTo T8s+ 98s
	Shove 10.9% TT-33 A8s+ ATo+ KJs+ QJs+ JTs
BB (20 big blinds)	Shove 20% 33+ A4s+ A8o+ K9s+ KTo+ Q9s+ JTs
UTG (98 big blinds)	Call 63.2% 22+ Qx J2s+ J4o+ T2s+ T6o+ 92s+ 96o+ 82s+ 85o+ 72s+ 75o+ 62s+ 64o+ 52s+ 54o 42s+ 32s

No surprises that UTG calls with all the hands they opened, but the rest of the table has to be selective because they have UTG left to act. When one of the remaining players shoves to isolate the Cutoff, that is a great result for our four big blind Hero, as it means the pot is likely to get heads-up against just one opponent with dead money in the middle. If the Button and Small Blind choose to flat, UTG could shove back over the top of them to isolate (or to try and win two bounties), a great result for the short stack, potentially getting a bigger pot against just one wide range. The Big Blind shoves their entire range when it is folded to them after a Cutoff shove because with no more bounties to win, their best shot at the bounty is to isolate and get the hand heads-up.

Things do change when we look at the same table makeup, but at the start of a PKO when nobody has been eliminated yet. As you will recall, the chip leader can open 100% of their hands profitably. Let's see how the table should respond when we do open any two:

How should table respond to UTG open	
Player	*Range*
UTG +1 (35 big blinds)	Call 38% K6-K2o Q4s Q2s Q7o-Q2o J5s-J2s J8o-J2o T5s-T2s 95s-92s 95o+ 84s-82s+ 85o+ 74s-73s 74o+ 63s-62s 64o 42s+ 32s Shove 43.1% 22+ Ax K2s+ K7o+ Q5s+ Q3s Q8o+ J6s+ T9o+ 96s+ 85s+ 75s+ 64s+ 54s
MP1 (30 big blinds)	Call 32.7% Q7s-Q6s Q7o-Q5o J8s-J3s J7o+ J4o-J2o T4s+ T7o+ T5o-T3o 92s+ 95o+ 85s+ 83s+ 85o 75s+ 76o 65s+ 52s 43s Shove 49.2% 22+ Kx+ Q8s+ Q5s Q3s-Q2s Q8o+ Q4o-Q2o J9s+ J2s J6o-J5o T3s-T2s T6o 84s 75s-74s 64s 53s+ 54o
MP2 (10 big blinds)	Shove 100% Any Two
MP3 (6 big blinds)	Shove 100% Any Two
CO (4 big blinds)	Call 55.1% 77-22 A7s-A2s A9o-A2o K9s-K2s KJo-K2o QTs-Q9s Q7s-Q2s QJo Q9o-Q2o JTs J8s-J2s JTo T9s T7s-T2s T9o-T6o 75o+ 65o Shove 15.9% 88+ A8s+ ATo+ KTs+ KQo QJs Q8s J9s J9o T8s+ 98s 87s 76s 65s 53s+
BU (25 big blinds)	Shove 35.9% 22+ Ax K4s+ K8o+ Q7s+ Q9o+ J8s+ J9o+ T8s+ 98s
SB (40 big blinds)	Call 50.6% TT-77 A8s-A5s A7o-A6o A4o K6s+ K2o+ Q8s+ Q4s-Q2s Q3o+ J2s+ J6o+ T2s+ T6o+ 98s 96o+ 86o+ 76o 65o Shove 19.3% JJ+ 66-22 A9s+ A4s-A2s A8o+ A5o A3o-A2o K5s-K2s Q7s-Q5s 97s 86s+ 75s+ 65s 54s
BB (20 big blinds)	Shove 100% Any Two

This time around we are facing a lot more shoves, because we have the widest range possible, so a similarly wide reshoving range performs very well. It also gets enough folds, believe it or not. As UTG we snap call with any two cards against the 10 big blinds or fewer stacks, and against the 20 big blind stack we call 50% of the time. Against the bigger stacks we have to fold more. This may seem like we are exploiting ourselves, but against half the table we can profitably call off more than half the time, so it makes it still a great spot.

The Cutoff is the interesting player here. As we have said before, as a short stack it is best to get it in against a wide chip leader because our hand performs well against the widest range and their presence protects us from a third player getting involved. That remains true here, but the 4 big blind Cutoff cannot get it in as wide as the 6, 10 and 20 big blind stacks who all can shove any two cards when folded to them. In the case of the 6 and 10 big blind stack, shoving ensures we get the smaller bounties if they come along, and in the case of the 20 big blind stack it's because we close the action and have some fold equity.

Most interestingly, the Cutoff calls more than they shove. This is because they have zero fold equity in this spot. By calling, we orchestrate a situation where somebody has to either reraise preflop or has to make a bet on the flop or later to get our bounty, which will have the secondary benefit of giving everyone else a chance to fold, getting us heads-up. If we shoved, it would likely set up a spot where one or more players flat then check down the hand, meaning we have to win multiway.

One last thing to note is that even though UTG is supposed to open any two, if they do fold preflop then UTG+1 can profitably open any two, if they happen to fold preflop, MP1 can also profitably play any two cards. This is because they are the next biggest stacks at the table and thus can bust the most people, which hammers home the important point that when you are the de facto chip leader every spot becomes more profitable. For this reason, we have even pondered whether it is a profitable game plan to take a minus EV flip the first hand of a PKO just because the times we do win, we set up some incredibly profitable spots every hand after (If you ever play Hyper PKO SNGs you will see a lot of the winning regs gamble early to do just this).

The table set up we have just seen in this example we carefully selected because it shows some extremes, but any example you study away from the tables is going to be just as complex, especially when you compare them to normal tournament equivalents. This is why we implore you to observe the key adjustments and the broad takeaways, rather than trying to use these examples as a template.

Key takeaways

- When stacks are shallow and you cover your opponents, shoving, rather than limping or min raising, is optimal because it means you are guaranteed a bounty when you win
- Players in early position can call shoves wider when they can win the bounty from players in later position
- When you are the table chip leader min raising is often an optimal strategy because your upside is greater than everyone else's
- When the chip leader raises, if you cover the players behind you, you are usually better off calling to keep them in the pot
- Taking on the chip leader is usually your best option as a short stack, they have the widest range and the bigger stacks will stay out of your way
- You can often play 100% of hands profitably as the chip leader

Chapter 12. Mental game

What perhaps makes PKOs unique is that the presence of ICM and bounties pull you in two different directions. Sometimes you have to take a seemingly crazy risk to win bounties and other times it is better to err on the side of caution because the payouts are more important. This balancing act and the level of complexity it often creates is probably why PKOs will never be a truly solved form of poker and also why they are profitable. This does mean they will likely create some mindset issues that you might not be used to in any other format.

I don't want to do a deep dive into how to resolve these mental game issues. For that I would point you to *The Mental Game of Poker* by Jared Tendler of which I am a big fan (but to point out an obvious bias where this is concerned, my co-author Barry is also the co-author of that book). I also often suggest to my students *Thinking Fast & Slow* by Daniel Kahneman, which has a large section on cognitive biases that will impact your own mental game issues. It is useful right now to point out some of the mental game issues you will encounter in PKOs, so you can pre-empt them, recognise them for what they are, seek help to resolve them and also so you know you are not alone as *most* poker players experience these problems in PKOs.

One final point, before we get to the specific issues, is that 90% of mental game problems like this can be overcome with experience. The more you understand PKO strategy, the easier it is to recognise when you got unlucky or when you made a mistake. Jared Tendler also says this early in his book, that improving technical knowledge is usually the best way to prevent tilt. Before you jump to the conclusion that you need a shrink, spend some time reviewing your hands and maybe practising with PKO SNGs to solidify your strategy. Beyond that, these are the mental game issues you will encounter in PKOs.

Not knowing what to do

The biggest mental game issue that good players have in PKOs is simply having to deal with so much uncertainty. Serious poker players can deal with making the right decision but still losing, but not knowing whether they made the right decision is stressful. If you are a solid MTT player you will know instinctively what to do in most spots and if not you can make a note of the hand for review later. That is simply not possible in PKOs, if you play 10,000 hands of PKOs there might be 500 where you did not know what to do. In a normal MTT the tough decisions are close anyway, the difference between calling and folding might only have a small impact on your bottom line. But because the prizes are so top heavy in PKOs a small mistake could have a huge impact on your profitability.

In a normal MTT we would advise using moments of uncertainty for growth and that is still the case in PKOs, but unlike regular MTTs you are going to have to tolerate not knowing as much as you would in a regular MTT.

We are lucky enough that Jared Tendler of the aforementioned *Mental Game of Poker* took some time out to address this particular issue for us:

There is a practical component to dealing with the uncertainty related to the game itself. PKOs are a new and complex format so of course there will be big gaps in knowledge. Studying spots more, reading this book, doing simulations and discussing hands with fellow players is your best bet for solving for this uncertainty.

Many of you will also have to deal with an emotional overreaction that comes from a flawed assumption about uncertainty. Ask yourself what you hate about not knowing all the answers? Hatred of unknowns could come from a confidence issue. Doubt that you can figure it out, for example. Good players gain stability in their confidence simply from knowing they will eventually figure these spots out, even if they can't right now. Some players hate making mistakes and assume if they lose it's because they made a mistake. PKOs make it hard to distinguish between mistakes and good decisions that went unrewarded, but assuming losses mean you were wrong undermines confidence.

You will create more certainty the more you study PKOs and know that everybody who plays them is experiencing the same thing, they are still very much an unmapped territory. Beyond that if you are still struggling to deal with the not knowing, check out the confidence chapter of my book The Mental Game of Poker.

Decision paralysis

The more immediate impact of not knowing what to do will be decision paralysis. This is where having too many options or too many things to think about will actually shut down your ability to think in the moment. In a PKO you may find yourself in bizarre situations, which would normally be an easy fold in a regular MTT, where you are contemplating calling a three-way all-in with 48 suited and you have two opposing forces (ICM and the bounties) forcing you into a stalemate.

As we just mentioned you simply cannot mark every PKO hand for review, but first and foremost these moments that bring you to a literal standstill are indeed the ones you should be reviewing after you finish your session. Not only do they represent a big knowledge gap you can fill they are costing you EV in the form of your timebank. After the hand, mark the hand history for further review to stop this happening in similar future spots.

But how do you get yourself out of that frozen state in the moment where you perhaps only have 20-30 seconds in your timebank? Jared Tendler again:

If you are regularly timing out because a spot has you stumped, I recommend creating what I call a 'Strategic Reminder', which is basically just a prompt on a piece of paper or a note on your phone to remind you what a good decision looks like, in this case in the context of PKOs.

For example, write out maybe the four or five most important foundational things you have taken from this book that you are currently working on. In the early going that should certainly include your equity against standard ranges and the Bounty Discount tables. On top of that, just make a short note about the biggest mistakes you have been making that you don't want to repeat.

Use the Strategic Reminder as a prompt for good decision when you otherwise would freeze. With so much uncertainty it's useful to have something known you can hang your hat on in those critical moments.

Once you find yourself thinking about these things automatically in tough spots without using the reminder, you can move on to the next areas for improvement. That's a sign you have mastered aspects of your decision making that you were previously struggling with and now you can incorporate something new.

Hating gambling

Beyond the uncertainty, the unique way that PKOs torture you mentally is from the increased variance and volatile nature of them. As a poker player you know what it's like to play your best for four hours then getting your money in the middle of the table with a coin flip hand, but in PKOs we are routinely getting all the money in the middle of the table profitably with any two cards.

It was stated at the outset of this book that one of the reasons that PKOs are currently profitable is because not only do they attract weak players but many good regulars often avoid them because they have too much gamble in them. The players who avoided PLO because of the variance steer clear of PKOs for the same reason (I know a lot of good PLO players who are naturals at PKOs). So if you are a good player there is a decent chance that your biggest problem with PKOs is you cannot bring yourself to take the necessary risks needed to win the juicy bounties.

First and foremost, an immediate and important adjustment would be to ensure you are bankrolled adequately for PKOs. You need a bigger bankroll for PKOs because although you min cash more the final table prizes are much more top heavy. So if you are a regular in $22 MTTs, maybe play $11 PKOs. This simple adjustment is not only correct for your bankroll it will also make it easier to roll the dice when you need to.

Jared Tendler:

If you take strategic risks, that's not gambling. Gambling is a risky bet with a negative return. To suggest you hate gambling implies the game is gambling, when the opposite is true — you've learned that better players actually have a big edge in this game. While short-term results may feel like the outcomes are purely based on luck and not skill, that's not true in the long run.

If you hate gambling there may be a part of you that hates the game. If that's the case, you need to ask yourself, why are you choosing to play this format over others? If you are unsure, you need a clear answer otherwise this hole makes the ups and downs of this format feel even more like gambling.

If you haven't already, it might be worth taking a look at our book *Poker Satellite Strategy*. As counter-intuitive as it might seem, between satellites (which are incredibly tight) and PKOs (which are incredibly loose) you will learn about the extremes of ICM. This is what we like to call the 'ICM dial' which is a metaphor for how the presence of ICM means you should play tighter or looser in different situations. This book was born in part because we realised that you should often do the complete opposite in PKOs as you would in satellites. So one way to find your gamble in PKO tournaments is to take a holistic approach to ICM in general.

Gambling too much

You also have the inevitable overcorrection some other players will make of putting too much emphasis on the bounty element and the fact that ranges expand. Calling too wide when a big bounty is on the line is perhaps the most forgiving of the mental game issues listed here because the upside of winning is big, but it is still an issue. In particular this leak will materialise in the form of overcalling when the bounties are relatively low compared to what you are risking, especially if ICM has a big impact in this stage of the tournament.

Whether you hate gambling or gamble too much in PKOs, one inevitability of fixing your leak is you might overcorrect in the other direction. If you were playing too tight, when you correct this you might play too loose, and vice versa.

Like everything else in PKOs you have two opposing forces pulling you in different directions so see this, as well as your PKO study in general, as a constantly evolving thing. Never make the mistake of thinking you understand this balancing act or you will get pulled too much in one direction.

Entitlement Tilt

In the *Mental Game of Poker*, Jared identifies seven types of tilt that all poker players will experience. No doubt all of them come into play in PKOs, but one, in particular, stands out which is Entitlement Tilt. This is the tilt that comes from feeling like you 'deserve' to win more than your opponent, either because you work harder, are smarter or a better player, or you deserve a bit of good luck. I firmly believe all winning players have this entitlement tilt, we always root for the best player because we identify with the better player, we don't like to see 'donkeys' rewarded, even though it's good for the game.

This is more prevalent in PKOs because people will show up with hands they never would in any other format, win with them and often be right to have played them. There will indeed be a sense that other players are just gambling when they call with a bad hand, but you made a good strategic decision when you did the same thing.

One final time, Jared Tendler:

It makes perfect sense that the sense of entitlement will be high in PKOs, with so little information about PKOs out there, by simply buying this book you might feel you deserve to win because you have put some effort into getting better at them.

Don't forget that this is a game where you regularly will put your chips in the middle with 30% equity when you never would in a regular tournament. From a ChipEV perspective you are going to lose much more in PKOs than in other formats, it's just you will get compensated for it the times you do win. Finally, remember the fact recreational players get rewarded often in the short term is precisely what makes PKOs a profitable format.

To echo Jared's sentiment I shall end by pointing out that since I have specialised in PKOs, when I do bust from them the most common position I finish in is actually as the first player eliminated from the tournament. Just as bubbling satellites is a sign you are playing them well, being the first player out is a sign you are probably playing PKOs correctly, because you should be playing to win all the bounties and trying to get the chip lead early. So get the idea that you deserve to win out of your head, this is a format where you should get very used to busting out brutally and quickly.

Chapter 13 How to study pkos on your own

As we pointed out at the start, we see this book as a way to understand the key adjustments you need to make in PKOs compared to normal MTTs before you embark on further study. This book is by no means the only study you should put into your PKO game. As Progressive Knockout Tournaments evolve and get more popular, so will the literature around them, not to mention the solver technology. We still think this book will stand the test of time as a jumping-off point for PKO study but they will get more difficult, so the onus is on you to do more work away from the tables.

If you are going to take PKO study seriously then you are going to have to review hands using an ICM calculator that has been updated to include PKOs. We pondered including some hints and tips on how to best use these technologies but they get updated so quickly that any advice we would give would invariably date. In fact they got much more sophisticated while we were writing this book. At the time of writing the two best offerings on the market are ICMIZER and we personally recommend **Holdem Resources Calculator**.

One broad piece of advice we can give about using ICM calculators which will not date, and it was the method we used to write this book, would be to study your ranges using these tools in standard MTT spots and then comparing them to the PKO equivalent. So, for example, if you are considering your Button shoving ranges against two short stacks on the bubble, look at what they would be in a normal tournament first, then look at the same spot in a PKO, and pay particular attention to the adjustments. This will help you improve both your PKO game and at the same time your regular MTT game, as you will be studying your baseline ranges by default.

If you haven't already, please revisit the chapter on your equity against standard ranges. We really think this is the most important way you can develop a solid PKO game. Only when you have a really good understanding of what, for example, your equity is with JQs against a tight opening range, can you begin to apply the bounty discount. It's no good shaving 5% off the equity you need if you have no idea what equity you have in a standard ChipEV spot. There are a lot of great equity calculators out there to play around with, including a very good one that comes with PokerTracker.

Beyond the PKO material itself another consideration for further study is heads-up play. Although strategically the PKO factor doesn't come into the heads-up stage, the final payouts in PKOs are often much more than a regular MTT. As such, being proficient in heads-up play is going to yield big returns for you over the long term.

A student of mine, Lee Lawrenson, has produced a smartphone app which quickly calculates Bounty Factor if doing maths on the fly is not your thing. You can buy a copy by emailing him at **lee.lawrenson@yahoo.co.uk**.

As the game is ever-evolving and some spots are going to be insanely tricky, don't be shy if you have a question. Feel free to find me on Twitter @daraokearney if you have a difficult hand you wanted to get a second opinion on. And if you want a good laugh, you could ask Barry @barry_carter.

Finally, for extra free tips, be sure to join my mailing list where I send a regular strategy newsletter.

tinyurl.com/GTOPoker

Acknowledgements

We would both like to thank some of the people that helped us get this book over the line, including Kat Arnsby, Jared Tendler and Saron Harford. Thank you also to everyone at Unibet Poker, ShareMyPair and PokerStrategy.com for their support over the years.

We would really like to thank all of our advance readers for their feedback and suggestions, including Elron Steele, Lee Lawrenson, Sameer Singh, Carlos Welch, Gareth James, George Devine, Jason Tompkins, Jamie Nixon, Matt Skeadas and Gareth Chantler.

We would like to say a big thank you to Benjamin "bencb" Rolle, Collin Moshman, Michael Acevedo whose work we cite in this book. Thank you very much to Donna Morton, Clodagh Hansen, George Devine, Marty Mathis and Lara Neacy for all their help promoting the last book, we are sure you will do the same for this one.

And yes, we would both like to thank David Lappin for genuinely influencing the content this time around - there, we said it.

Barry would like to thank Gina, Sarah and Mum. As always, big thanks to Simon 'Jonesy' Jones for teaching me the game in the first place.

I'd like to thank my long-suffering, ever supportive, wife Mireille, my poker kids Jack Hardcastle, Jack Sinclair, Daragh Davey, Simon Steedman, Jamie Nixon, Polly Malone, Henry Kilbane and Alan Widmann, and my real life kids Paddy, Fiona and Oisin. I'd also like to thank my study buddies Sameer Singh, Monica Vaka and Jack Hardcastle who acted as a soundboard for many of my ideas, and my longest standing poker friends David Lappin, Daiva Byrne, Jason Tompkins, Daragh Davey, Sameer Singh and Ian Simpson. And a final thank you to Adam Owen for providing the cover quote.

The Authors

Dara O'Kearney

Dara O'Kearney is a professional poker player from Ireland with a long standing reputation as the best satellite specialist in the game as well as one of the great teachers of poker. He has won over $1 million in satellite tournaments alone and twice won the PokerStars UKIPT satellite leaderboard. He is sponsored by Unibet Poker and is the co-host of The Chip Race Podcast.

www.twitter.com/daraokearney
www.dokearney.blogspot.com

Barry Carter

Barry Carter is a poker author from the United Kingdom with a long standing reputation as a mediocre player. He is the editor of PokerStrategy.com, the world's largest poker community, and co-author of the best-selling books The Mental Game of Poker 1 & 2.

www.twitter.com/barry_carter
www.pokermediapro.com

Also by the authors

Poker Satellite Strategy
Dara O'Kearney's first book on how to qualify for live and online poker tournaments for a fraction of the price.

Buy Poker Satellite Strategy: http://mybook.to/satellite

Endgame Poker Strategy: The ICM Book
Dara & Barry write the first detailed book on ICM in regular tournaments which covers bubbles, post flop, laddering, deal making and much more.

Buy Endgame Poker Strategy: http://mybook.to/icm

GTO Poker Simplified
Dara and Barry return with their fourth book tackling their most difficult topic to date – GTO.

As the name suggests, this is the first book to boil down the lessons from the solvers to actionable and easy to digest lessons that any player can apply to their game.

Buy GTO Poker Simplified: https://mybook.to/GTO

The Mental Game of Poker
Barry Carter and Jared Tendler's best selling book on how to eliminate tilt and other mental game issues forever.
Buy The Mental Game of Poker: http://mybook.to/mental

The Mental Game of Poker 2
Barry and Jared's follow up which shows you how to play poker in the zone consistently.
Buy The Mental Game of Poker 2: http://mybook.to/mental2

Made in the USA
Las Vegas, NV
05 January 2024

83961497R00089